TEEN INCARCERATION
FROM CELL BARS TO ANKLE BRACELETS

PATRICK JONES

TWENTY-FIRST CENTURY BOOKS / MINNEAPOLIS

Twenty-First Century Books
A division of Lerner Publishing Group, Inc.
241 First Avenue North
Minneapolis, MN 55401 USA

For reading levels and more information, look up this title at www.lernerbooks.com.

Main body text set in Adobe Garamond Pro 11/15
Typeface provided by Adobe Systems.

Library of Congress Cataloging-in-Publication Data [BF]

The Cataloging-in-Publication Data for *Teen Incarceration From Cell Bars to Ankle Bracelets* at the Library of Congress.
ISBN 978-1-4677-7572-4 (lib. bdg.)
ISBN 978-1-5124-1138-6 (EB pdf)

Manufactured in the United States of America
1-37426-18418-4/15/2016

CONTENTS

INTRODUCTION

L ionel Tate was a twelve-year-old fan of professional wrestling. Like lots of kids that age, he liked to imitate wrestling matches he saw on the television screen, probably believing that what he was seeing wasn't real. At his home in Broward County, Florida, one day in 1999, he "play wrestled" with a six-year-old friend named Tiffany. The play turned violent, and Tiffany died from a fractured skull, lacerated liver, and more than thirty other injuries. Although he was only twelve years old, Lionel was arrested, charged as an adult with first-degree murder, and eventually brought to trial in adult court in 2001. According to Judge Joel T. Lazarus, who heard the case, Lionel murdered Tiffany in a way the judge described as "cold, callous and indescribably cruel." The murder shocked the nation but the sentence even more so: life in prison without parole. For an act committed before he was old enough to drive or to do anything considered adult, Tate was found guilty and sentenced in adult criminal court to spend the rest of his life behind bars.

Lionel's lawyers successfully appealed his sentencing on the grounds that he had not been evaluated for competence to stand trial in adult court. Lionel was released from prison in 2004 and placed instead on house arrest with a ten-year probation, which he quickly violated.

Lionel Tate, sixteen, and his mother, Kathleen Grossett-Tate, stand outside Broward County courthouse in Fort Lauderdale, Florida, on January 29, 2004, after he pled guilty to a second-degree murder plea bargain deal that set him free after nearly three years in prison. Tate was convicted of murder in the death of six-year-old Tiffany Eunick in July 1999 when he was only twelve years old.

Within a few years, Tate was arrested for armed robbery and sentenced to thirty years in a Florida state prison.

Almost all youth do stupid, impulsive things. Yet only some of them turn into criminal acts. Some youth get caught committing those crimes, some don't. Depending on the nature of their crime, some offenders might be sentenced to pick up trash for a day, while some rot away in cells for years. Lionel's case made headlines because of the horrific, violent nature of the crime but more so for the harsh sentence. Lionel took Tiffany's life before she had a chance to grow up. Florida did the same to twelve-year-old Lionel.

TRANSITIONS

In 2004, a few years after Lionel's case made national news, I began visiting Hennepin County's two juvenile correctional facilities: the Juvenile Detention Center (JDC) and the Hennepin County Home School (CHS). Located in Minneapolis, Minnesota, the JDC is a secure detention facility to hold arrested youth until their cases are decided. It has locked doors, guards, and other measures to ensure no one escapes. Depending on a juvenile court judge's decision, youth offenders might be allowed to return home, be placed in a diversion program outside of the justice system, or given an alternative to incarceration such as community service or electronic home monitoring (EHM). If the crime was violent, the youth was a repeat offender, or both, the youth will most likely stay in JDC until the trial. When I began visiting the eighty-seven bed JDC facility, it was almost always full. On some weekends, it was overcrowded, with residents sleeping in the gym. While there are no cell bars, JDC has a jail-like vibe, with locked doors, hard beds, and county-issued T-shirts and sweatpants. It's no place you'd want to be. Having to act tough all day in front of other residents, at night, alone in a cell, kids often break down in worry, terror, and remorse.

The CHS, in a western suburb of Minneapolis, is an example of an out-of-home placement where a youth might be placed after trial. Youth at CHS have been found by a juvenile court judge to be delinquent—that is, to have committed a criminal act. At the CHS, the youth offender does time (punishment) and participates in therapeutic programs (rehabilitation). Located on what was once a working farm, CHS had eight cottages in 2004, with beds for sixteen residents in each. One cottage housed girls, another held residents in the Juvenile Sex Offender Program (JSOP), and youth convicted mainly of gang-related crimes lived in the other cottages. Some of the girls and JSOP youth stayed a year at CHS, while most others served at least six months. A secure unit called the Crisis Intervention Unit (CIU) housed short-term residents with behavior issues, such as not following rules. In short, the CIU was a version of solitary confinement. A few weeks before

Electronic home monitoring (EHM) devices are typically worn around the ankle.

release from CHS to return to the community, residents moved to a transitional living space in the basement of the administration building. While not overcrowded like the JDC, CHS was almost always full. As soon as one resident transferred out, another would be placed in the facility.

A decade later, Hennepin County is in talks to merge the CHS with a similar facility in adjoining Ramsey County, which includes the city of Saint Paul, Minnesota. Rather than eight cottages and a transition unit, CHS now has only four cottages—none of them ever close to full—with most placements lasting only three to four months. JDC has several vacant floors and an average population of forty residents, most of whom stay for less than a week. Hennepin County has less youth crime, and fewer youth are locked up. For these reasons, fewer facilities are necessary for youth offenders. How can this be?

A NATIONAL TREND

The downward trend in youth crime in Hennepin County and the movement toward alternative placements for those who do offend is a reflection of what is happening across the United States in the twenty-first century. Under programs such as Hennepin County's Juvenile Detention Alternatives Initiative (JDAI), begun in 2006, a juvenile court judge is more likely to put a youth offender on electronic home monitoring than in secure detention. With EHM the youth wears an ankle bracelet that allows for remote supervision. This type of monitoring allows an offender to continue with schooling and other daily activities. The goal of JDAI is "to create an effective, fair, and efficient system that produces positive outcomes for youth, families, and communities while protecting public safety." If the crime is not serious, the judge may refer an offending youth to a diversion program or put the offender on probation. Both options involve sanctions (restrictions) but not placement in a facility.

Evidence shows that JDAI is working in Hennepin County and in other counties all over the United States. The evidence clearly demonstrates that locking most youth up has negative consequences for the youth when released, including recidivism (returning to criminal behavior). JDAI, rather than creating a vicious cycle of arrest and custody and rearrest, offers hope—not just to youth but to all of us who encounter young people in the juvenile justice system. Bottom line: the best way to keep youth out of the system long term is to never get them locked into it.

This book is based on my experiences with the juvenile justice system and on research about juvenile justice driven by the passage of the Juvenile Justice and Delinquency Prevention (JJDP) Act in 1974. This national legislation provides funding for local and state efforts to prevent youth crime and to improve the juvenile justice system, mostly by finding alternatives to placing youth into custody. In the decades since this landmark legislation, states and local jurisdictions (governments) have developed evidence-based practices that are improving the lives of youth and the health and safety of communities. The reforms have moved juvenile justice from systems based on fear of vicious, violent youth such as Lionel Tate—who make up only a tiny percentage of youth offenders—to those based on hard facts about youth development. These facts suggest that for most offenders, time in custody is counterproductive, that treating offending youth as adults has failed, and that harsh sentencing of youth doesn't work.

In this book, I'll be referring to youth offenders as youth or delinquents or kids, not as criminals. Author, journalist, and youth advocate Nell Bernstein observes that almost never in the juvenile justice system are the words *child* or *children* used, as if to hide that the young people in question are minors under the age of eighteen. This is an important distinction. By overlooking that children are in custody, people lose empathy and forget their own childhood misdeeds (which may have landed them in JDC). It also overshadows that children's brains are not fully formed, so they cannot be held fully responsible for their actions. These youth may have committed acts that are against the law, but that does not mean they are criminals by nature or "born bad."

BOTTOM LINE: THE BEST WAY TO KEEP YOUTH OUT OF THE SYSTEM LONG TERM IS TO NEVER GET THEM LOCKED INTO IT.

THE COLOR BAR AND THE GENDER DIVIDE

In this book, I'm writing mostly about black, Latino, and American Indian teen boys, many of whom are locked up in detention centers, reform schools, or prisons. So are white teen offenders, for whom—as with youth offenders of color—poverty, racism, broken schools, untreated trauma, and other factors beyond their control contribute to circumstances that lead them to commit crimes serious enough for them to be held in custody. Yet while minority kids make up about one-third of the US juvenile population, they are two-thirds of the juvenile corrections population. According to research conducted by the Annie E. Casey Foundation, "African-American youth are nearly five times as likely to be confined as their white peers. Latino and American Indian youth are between two and three times as likely to be confined. The disparities in youth confinement rates reflect a system that treats kids of color, particularly African Americans and Latinos, more punitively than similar white youth." The reasons for this vary, but it starts with who gets arrested. One recent study found that despite a drop in overall arrest rates, black youth in the United States are twice as likely to be arrested as white youth. Not just for criminal acts but even for minor offenses. For example, one study found that black youth were 269 percent more likely to be arrested for violating curfew laws than whites. This data shows disproportionate minority contact (DMC), or overrepresentation of minority youth, within the juvenile justice system.

DMC is not related only to detention and confinement. It is evident across most institutions and begins with school suspensions. In two of the larger school districts in Minnesota, for example, black students make up a minority of the student population but receive the majority of suspensions, beginning in elementary school. Some experts argue that DMC is the result of racial bias within the juvenile justice system. Others say DMC is the result of minority kids committing more crimes, more serious crimes, or the types of crimes that are more likely to lead to arrest and detention. Research clearly documents racial disparities in the juvenile (and adult) justice systems but offers no clear information on how or where it begins and how to end it. Yet experts point to a clear connection between education— or the lack of education—and

"I HAD BY THEN COMMITTED PETTY CRIMES IN ORDER TO FEED MY ADDICTION, BUT AFTER THAT, I ESCALATED TO SERIOUS BURGLARIES OF HOMES AND BUSINESSES, SINKING MYSELF EVER DEEPER INTO ADDICTION. AND THE MORE CRIMES I COMMITTED, THE MORE I REJECTED MY CONSCIENCE. IT WAS ALL ABOUT ME AND MY PAIN AND MY ANGER."
–JAMES, FIFTEEN

criminal behavior. They know that "about one in every 10 young male high school dropouts is in jail or juvenile detention, compared with one in 35 young male high school graduates." More kids of color are suspended, arrested, and put into custody because those same kids of color are falling into a widening achievement gap between how well they perform in school compared to white kids. Without access to quality child care, good integrated schools, and community resources, this gap will remain wide. And the rooms of JDC, CHS, and the Minnesota Correctional Facility–Red Wing (the juvenile prison in Minnesota) will continue to be filled with youth of color.

Female offenders often face different hurdles and harder barriers than males in the juvenile justice system. One correctional officer told me that in his thirty years of working with females in a short-term facility, almost every one of them had some history of untreated trauma, often sexual or physical abuse. A 2014 study of traumatic experiences in justice-involved youth found that "31 percent of girls reported a personal experience of sexual violence in the home, 41 percent reported being physically abused, and 84 percent reported experiencing family violence. Girls reported having been sexually abused at a rate 4.4 times higher than boys." Girls get into the system more through status offenses (truancy or breaking curfew) than through crimes against a person. And those who get into the system are kids of color. According to the same report, black girls are "20 percent more likely to be detained than white girls, while American Indian girls were 50 percent more likely." Overall, the number of girls arrested has increased, although the number detained remains at 15 percent.

While there will always be cases like Lionel Tate, in which youth commit terrible crimes, they make news because they are rare. For the vast majority of youth, their crimes are not horrific and don't merit harsh punishments. It seems like common sense, but it took policy makers in the United States years to figure out that sparing the rod does not spoil the child.

THE VICTIMS

The juvenile justice system begins with a crime committed against society, often against a specific person. The majority of the juvenile offenders profiled in this book have said that they began their real rehabilitation only when they focused on the victim or victims of their crime. The pain and suffering an offender experiences through harsh punishment and years of life lost behind bars cannot compare to a family whose loved one was harmed or killed as a result of an offender's actions.

The purpose of the criminal justice system, a warden at a Minnesota prison once told me, isn't to punish criminals—it is to prevent victims. The shift from punitive incarceration behind cell bars to developmentally appropriate punishment models stems from that same goal. The change is based on solid evidence that harsh punishments for most youth hurt not just the youthful offender but society at large. Harsh systems of punishment create more victims.

CHAPTER 1

HISTORY

I f famous literary characters such as Huck Finn, Tom Sawyer, or Oliver Twist had been pulling their antisocial antics in the United States in the mid-1990s, they'd probably be doing a year in a crowded publicly funded, privately run correctional facility complete with cell bars and razor wire. When they got out, chances are they would most likely reoffend since the emphasis during their time behind bars would have been on punishment and public safety, not rehabilitation and preventing recidivism.

In the US criminal justice system, the balance between punishment and rehabilitation has always been at play. One philosophy is to punish people for their crimes by locking them up and removing them from society so they can't commit other crimes. This approach theoretically improves public safety. A philosophy of rehabilitation, especially for youth offenders, is another key model. In this philosophy, society's role is to punish criminal behavior while also offering assistance (such as psychological therapy and addiction counseling) to help offenders change behaviors so they won't reoffend. In the rehabilitative model, jails, prisons, and other institutions for holding criminals are therefore called correctional facilities. Another key concept is proportionality of sentencing, meaning people are not given life in prison (a severe punishment) for stealing a loaf of bread (a minor crime).

Throughout US history, the pendulum between punishment and rehabilitation models has swung back and forth as society's mores change. One way of understanding the history of juvenile justice in the United States is to look at four distinct historical phases: social, legal, political, and scientific.

PHASE ONE: SOCIAL

The juvenile justice system in the United States is a fairly modern creation. In the early days of the country, after the United States won its independence from Great Britain in 1783, the criminal justice system typically treated children and adults who had committed crimes in the same way. Like adult criminals, youth offenders were flogged, jailed, or executed, depending on the severity of the crime. American society didn't view children, particularly teenagers, as a distinct or unique group. Like adults, youth went to war; worked the family farm; and in later centuries, toiled in factories. For the most part, early American rural society didn't believe in government solutions to crime and other social issues, so juvenile justice was typically handled by social figures and institutions, such as parents and church and community leaders.

US law mirrored English common law. The guiding text of that system of law was *Commentaries on the Laws of England* by William Blackstone, first published in the late 1760s. In this treatise, Blackstone noted that a person should only be held responsible for a crime if that person exhibited vicious will, or a knowing intent to break the law. Blackstone therefore believed that infants, defined as children under the age of seven, were too young to understand their actions and were not capable of committing crimes. In the eighteenth century, children over the age of fourteen were viewed as adults and treated accordingly by the law. The ages between seven and fourteen, however, were a gray zone from a legal point of view. Individuals who could be proven to understand the difference between right and wrong, and whose actions demonstrated vicious will, would be punished accordingly. In the case of a capital crime, this meant the death sentence. If intent could not be proven, a youth might escape severe punishment. As society progressed, harsh punishments, such as hanging an eight-year-old for stealing food, were increasingly viewed as inhumane.

In 1825 the Society for the Prevention of Juvenile Delinquency launched the nation's first effort to reform youth by building the House of Refuge in New York City. In addition to housing youth who had committed criminal acts, the House of Refuge also took in abandoned children. Half prison, half orphanage, it was a large, foreboding institution that housed hundreds of troubled youth. By the time of the Civil War (1861–1865), approximately twenty-five more reform facilities had opened throughout the country, almost all in large urban areas such as Boston, Massachusetts, and Philadelphia, Pennsylvania. The institutions offered shelter, food, and other basic needs of daily life. But because there were so many young people in each facility

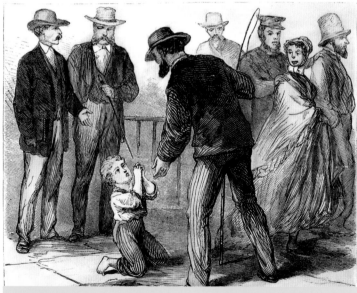

In this 1868 American wood engraving, a six-year-old boy, sentenced to the House of Refuge in New York City, pleads for mercy at a police court. His offense was vagrancy, or homelessness. Whippings and floggings were common punishments for criminal behavior at that time.

This illustration of life at the House of Refuge on Randall's Island in New York City appeared in *Harper's Weekly* in May 1868.

and few adult supervisors, the number one concern was maintaining control. Meant to help youth, the houses of refuge often hurt residents by placing vulnerable homeless kids with already hardened young criminals. This mistake would continue for the next 150 years.

In Chicago, Illinois, pioneering social worker Jane Addams offered another approach to youth crime. In her book *The Spirit of Youth and the City Streets* (1909), Addams argued that play and recreation programs—not just punishment—were needed to effectively combat delinquency. Wayward youth, as they were known at the time, were youth at risk of committing crimes or those who had already done so. Crime was caused, Addams and others believed, as much by societal factors, such as poverty, as by individual choice. Addams believed that wayward youth could be turned into productive members of society if provided with the opportunity. As the best method of crime prevention, she focused on establishing social programs at Hull House, a settlement house that she and social reformer Ellen Gates Starr cofounded in Chicago in 1889.

By the beginning of the twentieth century, psychology was an emerging science. It identified adolescence as a time in life when children are developing physically and psychologically into adults but are not yet afforded the rights or responsibilities of adults. Social institutions began to treat teens as a distinct group. The progressive movement of the era successfully pursued efforts to protect youth from exploitation. For example, new child labor laws set limits on workday hours and the age at which children could be employed. The laws also created compulsory education, requiring all children over a certain age to attend school. American society was increasingly viewing government as a force for improving and protecting the lives of citizens, particularly youth. Toward this end, the first juvenile court in the United States was founded in Cook County, Illinois (which includes Chicago).

Within a few decades, most states had a juvenile court system apart from the adult system. These courts were based on the British legal concept of *parens patriae*, in which the state, through its courts, has

Staff supervise an exercise class for boys at Hull House in Chicago in the early 1900s.

responsibility for looking out for the best interests of youth involved in criminal behavior. Juvenile courts of the time were informal and flexible. They functioned without the adversarial lawyer-against-lawyer approach of adult criminal courts. They were more about social work than criminal law, according to Julian Mack, an early juvenile court judge. He wrote,

> The child who must be brought into court should, of course, be made to know that he is face to face with the power of the state [government], but he should at the same time, and more emphatically, be made to feel that he is the object of its care and solicitude [concern]. The ordinary trappings of the courtroom are out of place in such hearings. The judge on a bench, looking down upon the boy standing at the bar, can never evoke a proper sympathetic spirit. Seated at a desk, with the child at his side, where he can on occasion put his arm around his shoulder and draw the lad to him, the judge, while losing none of his judicial dignity, will gain immensely in the effectiveness of his work.

The reform movement was based on the idea that youthful offenders were not bad people but rather youth who had done bad things. Guilt or innocence was not as important to reformers as was understanding why a young person had offended and finding ways to fix the problem. So, rather than being sent to a prison for punishment, youth offenders were sent to reform schools, ranches, or camps. These facilities, where youth learned skills to be productive members of society, were often outside of harsh urban environments and offered informal settings for training. That is, if a young person's case even made it to an impartial hearing. Often, in particular in the South, "justice" for kids of color such as the Scottsboro Boys was in the form of a rigged trial or a lynch mob. For most youth, however, up until the 1950s, the reform school model was the main way of dealing with youth offenders.

SCOTTSBORO BOYS

In 1931 nine African American youths between the ages of twelve and nineteen were arrested in Scottsboro, Alabama, for the rape of two white women on a train. The young men barely escaped a lynching by local citizens. The youths were quickly put on trial as adults—before all-white juries in Scottsboro. The juries quickly convicted the young men, and judges sentenced them to death, even though the youths had poor legal representation and no actual physical evidence of their guilt linked them to the rape.

The age of the ninth defendant—Roy Wright, twelve—gave his jury pause as they considered the death sentence. To impose capital punishment, a jury must come to a unanimous decision, and the jury in Wright's case did not do so, primarily because of his youth. The other eight sentences were eventually appealed, but only one was overturned soon after the trial, that of Eugene Williams. In 1932 the Alabama Supreme Court ruled that Williams should never have been tried as an adult because he was only thirteen at the time of the rape. Even in an era of overt and brutal racism, during which white southern juries were quick to find black defendants guilty on slim or no evidence, juries found it difficult to try, convict, and sentence young teens—regardless of their race—as adults.

Juanita E. Jackson (*fourth from left*) of the National Association for the Advancement of Colored People (NAACP) visits the Scottsboro Boys in Jefferson County Jail in Birmingham, Alabama, in November 1936. From 1935 to 1938, she was the organization's national youth director and special assistant to Walter F. White, the NAACP's executive secretary. The Scottsboro Boys were Andy Wright, Olen Montgomery, Roy Wright, Charles Weems, Ozie Powell, Haywood Patterson, Willie Roberson, Eugene Williams, and Clarence Norris.

REBELS WITH AND WITHOUT CAUSES

Juvenile delinquents were the subjects of many popular Hollywood movies in the 1950s and 1960s. Many of these films were poorly and quickly made B movies (now also known as direct to video). Yet some, such as *Rebel without a Cause* (1955), became classics. *Rebel* featured James Dean in an iconic role (with an equally iconic red jacket) as Jim Stark, a troubled young man. In the first scene, Jim is at a police station. He has been arrested for being drunk in public. At the station, he meets two other arrested youths with whom he will develop friendships: Judy (played by Natalie Wood), a young woman who has been brought in for breaking curfew, and Plato (played by Sal Mineo), a teen from a broken family who has been arrested for firing a weapon. The rest of the film explores the lives of the three delinquents as they sort through loneliness, broken homes, sexuality, and other tough issues.

James Dean starred as a delinquent youth in the 1955 film classic *Rebel without a Cause*. In the film, his character wears a white T-shirt, jeans, and black work boots to signal his rebelliousness.

Another classic film that is representative of the mood of the era is *The Wild One* (1953). Marlon Brando stars as Johnny Strabler, the leader of an outlaw motorcycle gang. At a dance, when a local girl asks him, "Hey, Johnny, what're you rebelling against?" the Brando character famously answers, "Whadda you got??"

Then the tide began to shift as crime began to rise. Ranches, industrial schools, and camps began to construct bigger buildings to house more youth behind cell bars. The settings became more formal and more institutional, surrounded by razor wire fences. As the facilities grew larger, the emphasis shifted from changing youth to controlling them. The reform school ideal of promoting positive change transformed into discipline-heavy warehousing, or locking up "bad kids" without programs to help them change.

> **"PEOPLE NEED TO REMEMBER THAT KIDS ARE STILL GROWING UP AND FIGURING THINGS OUT, AND THEY WON'T BE THE SAME FOREVER."**
> —CALVIN, SEVENTEEN

In the 1950s, music, films, and books of American popular culture reflected a shift, focusing specifically on teens and teen consumers. Rebellious teens and juvenile delinquents were often the subjects of pop culture. In 1954 *Newsweek* magazine famously ran a cover story titled "The Kids Grow Worse." The story captured the mood of the country in wondering why, suddenly, there were all these bad kids wreaking havoc. The 1960s saw an explosion in the national youth crime rate, especially in the inner cities. Clearly, the times were changing, but not for the better in the world of juvenile justice.

PHASE TWO: LEGAL

To curb the rising tide of drug use and teen crime in the 1960s, legislators across the nation passed laws to deal with actions known as status offenses. A status offense is conduct that is considered a crime because the offender is an underage minor. Truancy (not going to school), running away, underage substance use, and ignoring curfews are common status offenses. As teen crime rose across the United States, the American public and politicians began to turn away from the protective reform approach to youth crime. Increasingly, the US judicial system tried youth offenders as adults under the rules of the adult criminal court—yet without giving youth offenders the same protections as adult offenders. In this way, courts began to abandon their commitment to the concept of parens patriae.

Two Supreme Court cases led to the "treat them like adults" stance and shook the foundation of the juvenile court system. In 1961 sixteen-year-old Morris Kent was arrested and charged with robbery, rape, and other offenses in the District of Columbia. Kent confessed to committing the crimes. As an underage offender, he would ordinarily have been tried in juvenile court. But because of the serious nature of the charges, Morris was tried in adult criminal court, found guilty, and sentenced to thirty to ninety years in prison. His legal team appealed the decision, and in 1966, his case *(Kent v. United States)* reached the US Supreme Court. Before the justices, Kent's lawyer argued that during Morris's original arrest and detention, he had been denied his constitutional rights by having his case referred, without a trial, out of the juvenile court system and into adult criminal court. The court agreed, saying that in trying Morris as an adult, the District of Columbia court had also abandoned the principal of parens patriae. Writing for the majority opinion, Justice Abe Fortas said,

> The Juvenile Court judge . . . held no hearing. He did not confer with petitioner [the person requesting a legal remedy] or petitioner's parents or petitioner's counsel. He entered an order reciting that after "full investigation, I do hereby waive" jurisdiction of petitioner and directing that he be "held for trial for [the alleged] offenses under the regular procedure of the U.S. District Court for the District of Columbia." He made no findings. He did not recite any reason for the waiver. He made no reference to the motions filed by petitioner's counsel [the defense attorney]. . . . We do not consider whether, on the merits, Kent should have been transferred; but there is no place in our system of law for reaching a result of such tremendous consequences without ceremony—without hearing, without effective assistance of counsel, without a statement

FIFTH AMENDMENT

The Fifth Amendment to the US Constitution, ratified in 1791, establishes a variety of rights for people who are accused of criminal behavior. The amendment reads in full:

> *No person shall be held to answer for a capital, or otherwise infamous crime, unless on a presentment or indictment of a Grand Jury, except in cases arising in the land or naval forces, or in the Militia, when in actual service in time of War or public danger; nor shall any person be subject for the same offence to be twice put in jeopardy of life or limb; nor shall be compelled in any criminal case to be a witness against himself, nor be deprived of life, liberty, or property, without due process of law; nor shall private property be taken for public use, without just compensation.*

of reasons. It is inconceivable that a court of justice dealing with adults with respect to a similar issue would proceed in this manner. It would be extraordinary if society's special concern for children, as reflected in the District of Columbia's Juvenile Court Act, permitted this procedure. We hold that it does not.

The next year, in the *In re Gault* decision, the US Supreme Court built on the *Kent* case by ruling that juveniles in criminal courts have the same rights as adults. Fortas reasoned that there may be legitimate reasons for treating youth and adults differently. Yet youth facing legal processes and imprisonment are still entitled to all the safeguards guaranteed to adults under the due process clauses of the Fifth and Fourteenth Amendments of the US Constitution. The *Kent* case established the need for a trial to move a case from juvenile to adult

FOURTEENTH AMENDMENT

The Fourteenth Amendment to the United States was ratified in 1868, after the Civil War, to define citizenship rights and to establish equal protection of the law to all Americans. Section 1 of the five-part amendment reads,

> *All persons born or naturalized in the United States, and subject to the jurisdiction thereof, are citizens of the United States and of the State wherein they reside. No State shall make or enforce any law which shall abridge the privileges or immunities of citizens of the United States; nor shall any State deprive any person of life, liberty, or property, without due process of law; nor deny to any person within its jurisdiction the equal protection of the laws.*

court. The *Gault* decision held that within juvenile court, youth did not lose their constitutional rights. The underlying logic in both cases found the court moving away from the informal nature of the juvenile court system to the more formal adult model.

The lone dissenter in the Gault case, Justice Potter Stewart, wrote,

> Juvenile proceedings are not criminal trials. They are not civil trials. They are simply not adversary proceedings. Whether treating with a delinquent child, a neglected child, a defective child, or a dependent child, a juvenile proceeding's whole purpose and mission is the very opposite of the mission and purpose of a prosecution in a criminal court. The object of the one [proceedings with juveniles] is correction of a condition. The object of the other [proceedings with adults] is conviction and punishment for a criminal act.

At the time, the *Gault* decision was hailed as a victory for children's rights. Yet over time, it became the first step toward a harsher system of dealing with juvenile offenders. Stemming from *Gault* and later court decisions, along with a public outcry to curb crime, flexibility was out, law and order was in.

THE WAR ON CRIME

After the *Kent* and *Gault* decisions, larger numbers of youth were tried as adults. Courts and youth corrections facilities became clogged. Under President Richard Nixon's war on crime in the early 1970s, more youth were arrested for status and drug offenses. But even with more youth locked up, the nation's teen crime rate still soared. Lawmakers felt that youth crime was so great a threat and placed such high costs to society, that the situation required federal action. In 1974, therefore, the US Congress passed the Juvenile Justice and Delinquency Prevention Act.

The underlying principle of the JJDP was to place responsibility with the US government rather than with states for setting standards for dealing with youth and families in the juvenile and criminal courts. A balance between punishment and rehabilitation remained at the core of the law. The goals of the law were to develop and use effective methods of preventing and reducing juvenile delinquency. This would be achieved by developing programs that prevented delinquency and that also created alternatives to the traditional method of punishing youth. To achieve this, state and local governments needed more money and needed research to understand what worked. The role of the federal government would be to grant funds while also conducting and sharing research. However, private foundations led the charge that put the ideals of the JJDP into practice. It would take thirty years for this to happen.

PHASE THREE: POLITICAL

The new law set clear standards for reforming the system to keep youth out of it. It wasn't a perfect solution, however. When crack cocaine came into the inner cities in the 1980s as a cheap and easy-to-buy drug, communities—and the reform-based approach of JJDP—began to fall apart. Urban areas saw a rise in crime, much of it related to youth gangs selling crack. Gangs became public enemy number one, even though most of the violence was directed at other gangs and not at average citizens. With gangs came weapons, and gun violence among youth soared. Many Americans feared that gang-related cases, crimes by very young violent offenders such as Lionel Tate, and the rise of mass school shootings in the 1990s were signs that the rowdy juvenile delinquents of earlier decades were being replaced by something much worse: man-child monsters.

An August 1993 *Newsweek* magazine cover story reflected the mood of a scared nation in an article titled "Wild in the Streets." Beginning with the details of a horrific crime by a teen, the article suggested that youth violence in the United States was out of control and that the reform-based approach to teen crime was outmoded for the new breed of teen criminal. So almost every state changed its juvenile justice system, focusing on punishment and strict offense-based sentencing—all of which was contrary to JJDP. And in the early 1970s, President Richard Nixon had launched a so-called war on drugs, which initially targeted marijuana and by the 1980s the crack cocaine epidemic. Young people of color were most impacted by the epidemic. They were more likely to be arrested, convicted, and sent to the increasing number of prisons being built to serve the war on drugs and the increase in teen crime.

Experts fueled public fears by claiming that violent juvenile crime was not only increasing but would continue to soar. They said that juvenile super predators—a term adopted by some criminologists to describe the most violent youth offenders—were committing more violent crimes at a higher frequency than delinquents of the past. Looking at birthrate data, experts predicted these killing machines would overrun the nation. They felt that super predators were born criminals for whom rehabilitation was useless. Based on these theories, protecting the public from young psychopaths became the main concern of the juvenile justice system in the 1990s.

JJDP

The Juvenile Justice and Delinquency Prevention Act (Public Law 93–415), passed in 1974 and reauthorized periodically ever since, laid out the following concerns about juvenile justice issues in the United States:

(a) The Congress hereby finds that

(1) juveniles account for almost half the arrests for serious crimes in the United States today;

(2) understaffed, overcrowded juvenile courts, probation services, and correctional facilities are not able to provide individualized justice or effective help;

(3) present juvenile courts, foster and protective care programs, and shelter facilities are inadequate to meet the needs of the countless abandoned and dependent children, who, because of this failure to provide effective services, may become delinquents;

(4) existing programs have not adequately responded to the particular problems of the increasing numbers of young people who are addicted to or who abuse drugs . . .

(5) juvenile delinquency can be prevented through programs designed to keep students in elementary and secondary schools through the prevention of unwarranted and arbitrary suspensions and expulsions;

(6) States and local communities which experience directly the devastating failures of the juvenile justice system do not presently have sufficient technical expertise or adequate resources . . .

(7) existing Federal programs have not provided the direction, coordination, resources, and leadership required to meet the crisis of delinquency.

QUANTEL LOTTS

Like many youthful offenders, Quantel Lotts grew up fast, exposed at a young age to drugs, violence, and poverty. When he was eleven years old, he saw one of his uncles shot to death in a drug dispute. Drug addiction ran rampant in his family. His mother was a crack addict who went missing for days in his hometown of Saint Louis, Missouri. With drugs came violence, and Quantel's family members beat him regularly. Quantel says, "I was taught that most problems can be solved with violence."

> **"I WAS TAUGHT THAT MOST PROBLEMS CAN BE SOLVED WITH VIOLENCE."**
>
> —QUANTEL LOTTS

Quantel was frequently in trouble at school, where he received only punishment, never counseling. When he was fourteen, Quantel stabbed a stepbrother to death with a hunting knife in a fight that had escalated to deadly violence. Tried as an adult, Quantel was sentenced in 2002 to life without parole. While in a juvenile facility, he created a crude tattoo on his arm with the words *dead man*. He later said, "That's how I felt at the time, like I was already dead." Various appeals on his behalf failed. He remains incarcerated in a Missouri state prison. Yet he told a CNN reporter that he is hopeful that he will eventually be released.

However, the super predator model proved to be wrong. For a decade, between 1994 and 2004, the juvenile arrest rate for violent crimes fell 49 percent. At the end of that period, the rate of violent offenses among youth was at its lowest level since 1980. The image of juvenile super predators, like most monsters, was just an urban legend.

Despite this compelling data, the juvenile justice system treated an entire generation of youth offenders as super predators. Many young offenders were tried and sentenced as adults during these get-tough times. They received long sentences for minor crimes or got life for crimes committed at a very young age. States with capital punishment were increasingly imposing the death sentence on violent youth offenders. In states without the death sentence, children as young as thirteen were among the thousands condemned to die in prison. Boot camps, Scared Straight programs, and other get-tough approaches became popular. Where the juvenile justice system had once viewed rehabilitation of youth offenders as a means to a better society, politics and social anxiety at the beginning of the twenty-first century forced a focus on punishment. Cell bars, not social programs, were back as the answer. The year 1995 was a peak year. On an average day, just under 110,000 youth were locked up.

Yet within the first decade of the new century, Americans began to take a more scientific approach to youth crime, asking, What does the research say? What is the evidence? What is the connection between biology and behavior? Enter the fourth and current phase of juvenile justice: the scientific stage.

The get-tough laws of the 1980s and 1990s prioritized harsh punishment and got many criminals off the streets. But the laws also created two big problems. First, the cost of arresting, trying, and warehousing youth offenders strained state and local government budgets. In addition, the American public felt that the pendulum had swung too far too fast. Published in 2001, a 1999 national study, for example, found that 80 percent of surveyed adults thought that rehabilitation should be the goal of juvenile corrections facilities. The same study revealed that more than 90 percent favored early intervention through after-school and Head Start (prekindergarten) programs to keep youth off the streets and out of crime. A backlash against the backlash meant the juvenile justice system was ready for reform once again. Having tried social, political, and legal methods, the American juvenile justice system turned to a scientific approach, based on research.

GET TOUGH GETS IT WRONG

Among other things, research and lawsuits pointed out that juvenile facilities in the United States were overcrowded and unable to meet the needs—including personal safety—of youth offenders. In 2000 a lawsuit on behalf of youth in a South Dakota facility, for example,

In January 2016, President Obama banned solitary confinement for juveniles in federal prisons, such as this one in California. He also limited the amount of time adults can spend in solitary for a first offense, bringing it down from 365 days to 60 days. Advocates for this type of reform argue that solitary confinement causes undue suffering and anguish and violates basic principles of human dignity. Proponents of solitary confinement say it is a necessary tool for protecting other inmates and prison staff from violent, dangerous inmates.

found that residents were often locked in isolation cells for up to twenty-three hours a day, for weeks or months at a time. In 2003 investigators discovered physical and psychological abuse and neglect at two Mississippi training schools that lacked recreation, education, and even medical care for residents. Conditions in California facilities in 2004 were found to be deplorable—understaffed and unsafe. In almost every lawsuit, attorneys shared findings that most youth offenders were held in conditions that were "dangerous, ineffective, unnecessary, wasteful, and inadequate." The poor conditions led, in part, to high recidivism rates. In these conditions, rehabilitation seemed impossible. Even worse, research has found that incarcerated youth are at great risk for self-harm. Completed suicides are almost four times higher than those for youth in the general population. Something had to change, and someone had to lead the charge.

Enter the John D. and Catherine T. MacArthur Foundation along with the Annie E. Casey Foundation. These large and influential private foundations provided funding to states and local governments to help them develop new juvenile justice policies based on evidence. With this evidence, governments would know which approaches worked and which didn't. And as a result of scientific evidence, systems that had once treated youth offenders as adults gave way to handling youth in a developmentally appropriate way. In doing so, Americans saw huge decreases in the number of youth in custody: a 2.3 percent decrease from 1997 to 2006, then another 6.5 percent decrease from 2006 to 2010. In fact, the rate of decline every year from 2006 to 2010 was almost three times faster than from 1997 to 2006.

ADOLESCENT DEVELOPMENT

Criminal behavior is driven by many factors. Some are societal influences such as poverty, education level, and family history. Others are emotional reasons such as revenge, greed, and pride. But new neuroscience research based on brain scans has also linked crime with brain immaturity. This evolving research reveals that the teen brain is wired differently from that of an adult, resulting in significant behavioral differences. From a legal point of view, because the teen brain isn't fully mature, youth cannot be held fully accountable for many actions, including criminal behavior.

Teen behavior is often driven by poor self-control; increased risk-taking; emotional highs and lows; and vulnerability to negative peer, media, and neighborhood influences. Taken together, this is a stew for criminality. A person unafraid to take risks, who doesn't recognize boundaries, and who is easily swayed by negative influences is vulnerable to committing crime. In fact, studies show that the age of seventeen is the apex, or peak, of criminal behavior.

During adolescence, some risk-taking is normal, biologically driven, and a predictable result of peer influence. But in some cases, peers push peers to take dangerous risks ("I dare you") or to join a gang. While these choices result in criminal behavior, they may be unavoidable in tough neighborhoods. Here, gangs and criminals may have the respect and sometimes all the power in a neighborhood. Joining a gang is seen as a means of survival. Add the popular media's celebration of crime, gangs, weapons, and wealth, and at-risk youth get pushed over the edge.

Research indicates that at-risk youth are those who come from one- or no-parent homes, in particular those who live in poverty. Kids who frequently change schools, who go to low-performing schools, and who face few consequences for bad behavior are more likely to do poorly in school. And poor performance in school is a major risk factor for involvement in crime. Without an education, job prospects dwindle. Selling drugs, stealing, or other criminal activity becomes, for some, a viable lifestyle. The school-to-prison-pipeline stereotype of an at-risk youth moving from a schoolroom to a street corner and then to a jail cell is very much based in reality.

> "MY JOURNEY WAS WRITTEN BEFORE I EVEN JOINED THE GANG. . . . MY DESTINY WAS WRITTEN WHEN I WAS BORN INTO A CHAOTIC FAMILY. . . . BEING BORN INTO THAT, AS MANY OTHER KIDS GET BORN INTO IT EVERY DAY, IT'S LIKE LIFE IS ALREADY WRITTEN FOR US."
>
> —ADOLFO, SENTENCED TO LIFE IN PRISON FOR A CRIME HE COMMITTED AT FOURTEEN

JUVENILE DETENTION ALTERNATIVES INITIATIVE

Most youth are likely to mature out of crime—unless the justice system makes it difficult for a youth offender to move to a law-abiding adult life. For some youth, time behind bars is not a time to reform but to make new criminal connections. In fact, research shows that locking a youth behind bars is not a way to protect public safety. On the contrary, jail can become a compact crime college. Rather than being scared straight, youth behind bars can turn into hard-core criminals.

SCHOOL-TO-PRISON PIPELINE

"School-to-prison pipeline" is a phrase that sociologists use to describe the policies and practices that lead to kicking students out of school and eventually, though not necessarily intentionally, into the criminal justice system. Schools that have strict rules about behavior, excessive policing on school grounds by police officers, dress codes, and other restrictive rules often have high suspension rates.

Kids of color are more likely to be suspended and are more likely to do poorly in school than other students. They are also more likely to drop out of school. Arne Duncan, former secretary of the US Department of Education, said,

> The linkage between education, or a lack thereof, and incarceration is powerful. More than two-thirds of state prison inmates are high school dropouts. And an African-American male between the ages of 20 and 24 without a high school diploma or GED has a higher chance of being imprisoned than of being employed. . . . Our schools suspend roughly three and a half million kids a year, and refer a quarter of a million children to the police each year. And the patterns are even more troubling for children of color—particularly boys—and for students with disabilities. We cannot lay our incarceration crisis at the door of our schools. But we have to do our part to end the school to prison pipeline.

Zero tolerance disciplinary policies—in which schools suspend students for any and all offenses—are often the first step in a journey through the pipeline. These get-tough policies impact mostly minority students. This is particularly true in poor elementary schools with large class sizes and with less money for high-quality teachers, counselors, and up-to-date equipment and devices. Schools with few or no school counselors and other support staff are unable to help youth deal with truancy and other issues that get in the

ZERO TOLERANCE DISCIPLINARY POLICIES . . . ARE OFTEN THE FIRST STEP IN A JOURNEY THROUGH THE SCHOOL-TO-PRISON PIPELINE.

In 2014 high school students in Detroit, Michigan, march to the state capitol in Lansing to protest policies that suspend or expel students for minor offenses such as not bringing their identification card to school. Get-tough policies such as these are disproportionately directed at students of color and often pave the way into the criminal justice system.

way of success. Instead, students are punished or expelled rather than receiving the help they need to improve and change behaviors. If expelled for even just one mistake, a young person in a poor, tough neighborhood can easily end up with a gang on the streets first, juvenile detention second, and prison next. If they even survive the dangers of gang life.

Much of this research was funded by the Annie E. Casey Foundation, which launched the multiyear Juvenile Detention Alternatives Initiative in December 1992. The Casey Foundation research, along with other studies, showed that mass incarceration wasn't working. For example, studies on recidivism found that juvenile facilities weren't placing youth on the path to success. Reoffending rates for young people released from juvenile correctional facilities across the nation were high. One study found that within three years of release, about 75 percent of youth were rearrested. About 45 to 72 percent were convicted of new offenses. In New York State, 89 percent of boys and 81 percent of girls released in the early 1990s were rearrested as adults before the age of thirty. While many of these were related to violating probation, the majority were for new crimes.

Locking up young people behind bars is also ineffective for youth offenders who have committed less serious crimes. In an Ohio study, low- and moderate-risk youth in correctional facilities were five times more likely to be incarcerated for later offenses than similar youth in alternative programs. In a 2007 Florida study, low-risk youth locked up with more violent criminals reoffended at a higher rate than similar youth who remained in the community on house arrest or another similar alternative. And they also reoffended at higher rates than high-risk youth placed in correctional facilities.

Research also showed that incarceration—especially stays over one year—reduces a young person's future success at school and in finding a job. One study found that correctional confinement at the age of sixteen or earlier leads to a 26 percent lower chance of graduating from high school by the age of nineteen. Other studies show that incarceration during adolescence results in substantial and long-lasting reductions in employment. These teens are more likely to reoffend as adults. So teens going to prison don't face a vicious cycle—they face a downward spiral.

Between 1997 and 2007, the total number of US youth in residential facilities declined 24 percent. The total of those incarcerated in long-term secure correctional institutions plummeted 41 percent. And even with fewer incarcerated kids, juvenile crime rates actually declined across the board, with a 27 percent drop in juvenile arrests for serious violent crimes.

WHAT DOES IT COST?

Incarceration is expensive. According to the American Correctional Association, the average daily cost nationwide to incarcerate just one juvenile offender is $241. Nationwide, according to a 2014 study, taxpayers spent almost $21 billion to confine youth offenders in juvenile institutions. In fact, most states spend the bulk of their yearly juvenile justice budgets on correctional institutions and other residential placements. Research has found that locking up youth costs more and doesn't reduce youth crime. Detention alternatives—such as EHM or community service—cost less and work better.

FLORIDA'S REDIRECTION PROGRAM . . . PROVIDES FAMILY-FOCUSED TREATMENT AS AN ALTERNATIVE TO DETENTION FOR LESS SERIOUS YOUTH OFFENDERS.

Florida's Redirection Program, for example, provides family-focused treatment as an alternative to detention for less serious youth offenders. In the family treatment approach, youth offenders are not locked behind bars but stay in their homes. Rather than working with correctional officers, youth and their families interact with social workers, therapists, and other human service professionals. The goal of this type of intervention is to work out family issues such as communication, chemical dependency, and other risk factors. Research has found that participants in the Florida program are much less likely to be arrested for a new crime, convicted of a new felony, or sentenced to an adult prison than similar youth placed in a juvenile correctional facility. And the Florida program saved money— more than $50 million over five years—through reduced costs and lower spending to prosecute and punish subsequent crimes.

WHAT WORKS?

By 2014 most states and hundreds of local governments, such as Hennepin County in Minnesota, had adopted JDAI as a way to cut spending on juvenile justice and to reduce crime and make communities safer. JDAI programs led to an increase in the number of youth referred to community-based resources such as community coaching and safe shelter programs, evening reporting centers, and electronic home monitoring. They allow offenders to stay in school, keep teen offenders from being pulled deeper into the system, and save taxpayers hundreds of thousands of dollars.

The MacArthur Foundation's Models for Change project created successful models of juvenile justice reform in four states (Illinois, Louisiana, Pennsylvania, and Washington). Models for Change hoped to transform juvenile justice by looking beyond detention alternatives. This project looked at larger issues. These included the link between youth in the juvenile justice system and in the welfare system, the need for strong legal defense for youth, and a response to mental health issues to keep youth out of trouble. New programs in these and other areas of juvenile justice were so successful that other states soon followed suit. Some states reformed their entire juvenile system. Mississippi, for example, outlawed the detention of status offenders in favor of community-based alternatives such as electronic home monitoring. Illinois created a juvenile corrections department separate from the adult system. Connecticut ended the practice of automatically prosecuting sixteen- and seventeen-year-olds in adult court. Virginia changed its "once an adult, always an adult" law, in which any youth charged in adult court, even if not convicted, would be tried as an adult for any future crimes.

Many states limit incarceration of youth to those who have committed serious offenses and pose a risk to public safety. Texas and California passed a law that allows residential placement only for young people found guilty of serious crimes known as felonies. Other states outlawed sentencing for low-level offenses except for youth with serious histories of prior offending. Almost every state changed the get-tough laws they had passed in the 1990s.

SAFER FOR EVERYONE

For kids who are locked up, the need for better conditions is clear. In the past four decades, recurring violence, abuse, and maltreatment have been documented in youth corrections facilities in almost every state. In 2010 the first national study on sexual abuse in juvenile correction facilities found that 12 percent of confined youth—more than three thousand young people—reported being victimized sexually by staff or other youth in their facilities. A 2008 Associated Press story found that thirteen thousand claims of abuse had been reported from 2004 through 2007 in juvenile facilities nationwide. In a 2010 survey of confined youth, 42 percent said they were somewhat or very afraid of being physically attacked, 45 percent said staff used force against youth when they didn't need to, and 30 percent said that staff placed youth in solitary as a form of discipline.

To address safety issues, Florida, Hawaii, Maryland, Mississippi, and New York expanded oversight of and improved safety conditions in facilities. Stronger background checks of staff and volunteers, eliminating "blind spots" where staff are unable to view all inmates in common areas, staff education, and other measures can reduce inmate abuse. Florida closed all boot camps—notorious for violence toward inmates—and outlawed "harmful psychological intimidation techniques" such as isolation, humiliation, and verbal abuse commonly used in the camps. Mississippi passed a law that said no first-time, nonviolent youth offender should spend more than ten days in a detention facility, where that offender would be likely to face violent or negative influences or both.

One of the biggest success stories has been to move incarcerated youth out of large buildings with many inmates and few therapeutic opportunities to small, treatment-oriented facilities. Massachusetts started this trend by shutting most of its reform schools in the 1970s.

REGINALD DWAYNE BETTS

At school, sixteen-year-old Reginald Dwayne Betts, called Dwayne, was an honor student, class officer, and an avid reader. But he was also restless. The restlessness led to drug use, truancy, and eventually crime. One night in 1996, Dwayne and a friend went joyriding in a stolen car in their hometown of Springfield, Virginia. Dwayne admits the behavior was totally out of character for him. He's unclear about the reasons for taking part but blames some of it on peer pressure. Mostly, his choice was ruled by poor decision-making skills due to a still forming teen brain.

Dwayne had a gun with him. Coming across a man asleep in a car, Dwayne pointed the gun at the man and stole his wallet and the car. Dwayne was quickly arrested and tried and found guilty as an adult. For this first offense, he received a sentence of nine years in prison.

Reginald Dwayne Betts is a published writer and a law student at Yale University. His most recent book is a collection of poetry entitled *Bastards of the Reagan Era* (2015). The title reflects his feeling that many of the harsh sentencing policies that came out of the years when Ronald Reagan was president created a generation of lost youth. Betts says that reading while in prison, particularly while in solitary confinement, turned his life around.

While in prison, Betts dedicated himself to self-improvement, taking advantage of educational opportunities, especially writing. Betts said, "I thought being a writer was one thing you could do while you were in prison, one thing you could develop and take home with you. I just didn't know I would be any good at it. From the very beginning, I was writing essays, reading books. I knew that that was the thing I was holding onto—I just had no idea how the world of writing and literature would open up to me." Write he did, authoring and publishing in 2010 an award-winning memoir called *A Question of Freedom: A Memoir of Learning, Survival, and Coming of Age in Prison.*

Betts is no longer in prison. He continues to write, focusing on poetry, and he speaks at juvenile detention centers and youth corrections facilities around the nation about his experiences. He's also enrolled in law school, and in 2012, Betts became a member of the Coordinating Council on Juvenile Justice and Delinquency Prevention.

Missouri began eliminating its large facilities in 1983. Instead, youth went into small facilities near their homes, which allows for supportive family contact. The largest have beds for fifty offenders, while the newer facilities can only house thirty-six. In these small settings, offenders receive group therapy, education, and any other services required in an individualized case management plan. With this small-is-better approach, Missouri's reoffending rates fell far lower than other states. Other states soon followed Missouri's lead. One expert commented, "I think it's clear that smaller, more therapeutic, closer to home, more involved with families, using staff supervision, eyes-on supervision and engagement with youth as the main provider of security, rather than the threat of isolation and punishment or restraint—that works much better than a more correctional approach."

CHAPTER 3
DETAINED

More than seven hundred thousand young people under the age of eighteen are arrested in the United States every year. They are arrested for a variety of reasons, from simple status offenses (such as breaking curfew) to misdemeanors (less serious crimes such as shoplifting) to felonies (such as rape and murder). Those caught in the act of a crime are arrested on the spot. In other situations, a suspected offender may not be on the scene of a crime when authorities arrive. Police can sometimes use a court order called a pickup order to track down and bring a suspect to court.

The police pick up and take the juvenile to a local police station for processing. This might involve contacting parents, an attorney, and a juvenile probation officer. It might also involve seeking medical care for the youth. Depending on the offense, standard procedures can also include booking, fingerprinting, photographing, and reviewing the circumstances of the arrest. The law in most states allows for a youth to be detained at a police station for up to six hours. Meanwhile, the police or county prosecutor (a lawyer who represents the county government) or both will decide the next steps. In many cases, particularly status offenses, the authorities will call parents or guardians to the police station. If the offense is minor and the youth has no previous criminal record, the authorities may give a simple warning and

Risk factors, such as poverty and troubled families, are the same for both offending teen boys and girls. However, girls are far more likely to be arrested for running away and for prostitution than are boys. Girls make up more than half of such arrests.

send the youth home. For low-level crimes such as curfew violation or shoplifting something worth a small amount, the officials may write a formal citation, which requires the person to appear later before a judge. For offenses such as vandalism, theft, drug possession, or other crimes not involving another person, the authorities may choose to submit the case to juvenile probation. This decision would lead to probation—a period of time where a youth's actions are supervised—or to community service. For more serious offenses such as assault, rape, and murder— which involve other people—formal charges will be filed and officials will fingerprint and photograph the youth offender. Those offenders are the most likely to be detained (held in prison) pending appearance before a judge. Deciding who is detained is most often determined by an objective tool rather than the subjective view of someone in the juvenile justice system. It makes the system fairer.

RISK ASSESSMENT

A new tool to guide whether an arrested juvenile is detained while that person awaits adjudication (a verdict and sentencing) is a risk assessment instrument (RAI). An RAI is a written guide that helps officials decide objectively what kind of response to criminal behavior makes the most sense in any given situation. The first part of the RAI ranks every crime with a score of 3 (the least serious) to 15 (the most serious). Crimes with a 15 rating—such as murder, assault, rape, and kidnapping—require that the juvenile go before a judge, who will determine if detention is needed. Crimes with a 6 rating—such as domestic assault and stalking—may require a mandatory judicial hearing, while others do not. Shoplifting and other crimes with a 3 rating are misdemeanors. In and of themselves, these crimes don't require a hearing but are added into the overall score. The RAI does not typically rank status offenses.

The second part of the RAI includes other factors to help officials determine the risk to the community of not detaining the youth. Each of these factors, mostly related to a youth's age and previous encounters with the juvenile justice system, has a score. Does the youth have a prior felony? If so, 6 points. A previous misdemeanor? Then 3 points. Has the youth failed to appear before a judge in the past? Does the youth have a pending case? Is the youth regularly going to school? The intake officer at the police station or detention center totals the score. In most cases, a person scoring 0 to 10 is released. Someone with a score of 11 to 14 receives a detention alternative such as electronic home monitoring. Those scoring over 15 will be detained in a juvenile detention center while they wait for a formal detention hearing.

LIFE AT JDC

If detained in Hennepin County, a youth is assigned to a room in a living unit at the Juvenile Detention Center. The assignment hinges not on age but on RAI risk factor totals. Youth offenders who score low will be placed in a unit with offenders who have similar scores. This prevents teens who are detained for striking a parent (domestic assault) from being held with teens who have committed more serious crimes, such as those involving a weapon. Youth offenders who score high are placed together, and these units are more carefully supervised. Often detained youth have gang affiliations and several gang members may be charged with the same crime. In these cases, detention officials will likely separate the gang members into different units so they have no contact with one another. Other offenders may require separation from others due to health issues.

In Hennepin County, the JDC units are called mods. Each mod has twelve small rooms, six on the top floor and six on the bottom floor. Girls are housed on a separate floor from the boys. The door to each mod is locked at all times, and doors to individual rooms are normally locked whenever a resident is inside. The room itself is small, with a bed, a shelf, a sink, a mirror, and a toilet. A common living area in each unit has tables, books, a few board games, and a TV. Youth have limited access to this room, based on behavior. Good behavior means more access. Bad behavior means less or sometimes no access. The facilities do not offer video games, Internet connection, or personal phones. Visitation is limited to occasional visits from family members and lawyers.

> **"NOBODY IS THERE FOR YOU OR CARES ABOUT YOU WHEN YOU ARE NOT LOCKED UP, BUT ONCE YOU ARE GONE, THEN THEY MISS YOU."**
> —ANGIE, SEVENTEEN

Young people eighteen years old and younger who have not graduated from high school or who do have general equivalency diploma (GED) certification attend the school at the facility. Youth older than sixteen are not legally required to attend classes, but they have little to do otherwise. During the day, offenders spend a lot of time standing in line, counting off to make sure everyone is accounted for, and walking silently in county-issued uniforms as they move between their mods and classrooms. Each day has a recreation period, during which youth visit a gym to play basketball or other sports. During warm weather, they play outside in an area with high walls. Youth from different mods don't pass one another in the halls, and only in very rare circumstances are they ever in the same room together.

Life in detention involves waiting, worrying, and wondering. Circumstances vary widely, but generally, most youth are detained for a few weeks. However, some detainees face delays, especially in the most serious cases or when lawyers and judges disagree about whether the case will stay in the juvenile system or move to adult criminal court. Not yet found guilty but certainly not free, juveniles in detention live in suspended animation.

THE DETENTION HEARING

Most detention hearings take place within a few days of an arrest. At a detention hearing, lawyers for the offender and for the government present evidence about the crime and about the young offender to a juvenile court judge. The judge considers the evidence to determine if the youth offender is a threat to public safety and likely to skip out on the next court appearance. If low risk and likely to cooperate, the youth will be released. If the youth is not a threat but the judge determines the person would benefit from therapy or other help, the youth is released with restrictions. The offender may be ordered into counseling or other treatment programs, for example. If the judge decides that the youth offender is a delinquent, the youth will be ordered to undergo examinations about mental health, substance dependency, and other issues to determine a therapeutic course of action. The youth may also face probation or be ordered to pay restitution (repayment) to the victim of the crime. If, on the other hand, the crime is extremely serious, the youth will stand trial.

If the youth offender faces trial, lawyers for the government enter formal charges at an arraignment. At this hearing, a judge will tell the defendant what the formal charges are, and the defendant and the defendant's lawyer will enter a plea of guilty or not guilty. Based on the severity of the crime, the judge will decide whether the case stays in juvenile court or is waived (moved) to adult court. In most states, some offenses such as murder require the judge to waive the case to adult court. The judge will also decide if the youth can be released before the case is fully resolved. If a young person faces trial in an adult court, for example, the youth will most likely go to an adult jail to await trial. In less serious crimes, where the youth is very young and has no previous criminal record, the judge will usually release the person. The offender promises to come back for trial, a disposition hearing, or any other court date that will wrap up the case.

DISPOSITION

If a youth's case stays in juvenile court, a disposition hearing is the next step. There, a judge decides what consequences are appropriate for the unlawful actions a youth has committed. Juvenile judges weigh a great deal of evidence, not just about the crime itself but about the youth charged with the crime. School records, family life, previous arrests, and other data guide a judge's decision. Most judges will focus on rehabilitation as the most appropriate sentence. If the youth is determined to be delinquent, the judge may settle on a placement, such as probation or juvenile prison. The judge determines the location and the length of time of the placement. Often the decision is related to the severity of the crime and how to best improve the youth's behavior.

Research shows that putting kids in custody does not deter crime, so fewer youth offenders are being locked up in any type of facility, even in reform schools. A 2015 census by the national Office of Juvenile Justice and Delinquency Prevention shows that the youth

Darwin Christopher Bagshaw *(far left)* attends a disposition hearing with his defense lawyer on July 31, 2015, in Salt Lake City, Utah. Bagshaw was accused of brutally beating to death his fifteen-year-old girlfriend, Anne Kasprzak, in 2012 when he was fourteen. Her body was dumped into a local river.

offender population in facilities for offenders dropped 14 percent from 2010 to 2012. The census also found that more youth offenders were in local facilities in 2012 than were in state-run facilities. Normally only the most violent and repeat offenders go to state-operated facilities. The census therefore suggests that locking up fewer youth has been successful in reducing recidivism and violent crime among youth offenders.

JORDAN

Jordan was thirteen years old when she first got in trouble in Johnson County, Kansas, for assault and destruction of property. She remembered being arrested and spending a night in juvenile detention, feeling scared and alone. Mostly, she recalled the smell. "It just smells like you're trapped. I will remember that smell for the rest of my life." Describing the experience of being admitted into detention, Jordan recalls the indignity of being stripped of her clothing and her belongings, and being left with nothing other than "a feeling of being violated."

Jordan's experience in detention did not change her criminal behavior, however. She continued to get into trouble, get arrested and detained, sometimes for days and other times for weeks. Since her crimes were not serious, she was released on probation. But Jordan would violate her probation and end up back in detention.

> **"IT JUST SMELLS LIKE YOU'RE TRAPPED. I WILL REMEMBER THAT SMELL FOR THE REST OF MY LIFE."**
> —JORDAN

Jordan lived in a jurisdiction that had implemented JDAI, so she had an opportunity to break the cycle of arrest and detention. Jordan's juvenile court judge believed in her and felt she had a drive to succeed. So the judge ordered that Jordan be placed in the Juvenile Intensive Supervision Program (JISP). JISP offer counseling, as well as frequent and highly structured contact with juvenile probation officers, among other features. Jordan credits the program with helping her to think positively about her future, which she hopes will include becoming a mentor for girls like her. Jordan says she knows that people learn from their mistakes, and she says, "I will always remember my story and will share it to help others."

CHAPTER 4

REFORMED

The first reform school in the United States, the Lyman School for Boys, opened in Westborough, Massachusetts, outside of Boston, in 1847. As a working farm in a rural setting, with multiple cottages and a large central building with a school, Lyman served as a model that many institutions followed. The cottages were like small prisons, housing altogether about one hundred youth. Residents went to school, performed chores on the farm, and learned a trade. Like most reform schools then, discipline was harsh and corporal (physical) punishment was common. Staff typically beat residents for breaking rules both major and minor. Reform schools flourished across the United States for the next 150 years.

LIFE IN A REFORM SCHOOL

The Glen Lake Farm School for Boys in Hennepin County, Minnesota, opened in 1909. The correctional facility is still in operation. It is called the Hennepin County Home School. With its rural setting, small housing units, and heavy emphasis on therapeutic programs, CHS represents the new direction in reform school juvenile programs. Rather than pitching hay, as residents would have done one hundred years ago, twenty-first-century residents exercise their cognitive skills (brain power) rather than their muscles to learn empathy.

Residents at the Lyman School for Boys, the nation's first reform school, work a farm field in the first decade of the twentieth century. Life at this reform school involved hard labor and physical punishment.

A CHS housing unit (called a cottage) has individual rooms and common areas, including a study room, a lounge, and a large dining area. Students get up for school, get dressed in their uniforms (long blue shirts), and walk single file from their cottage to the main school building. On the way, they pass the basketball hoop and maybe even a gaggle of geese. Except for a gate at the front entrance, the facility has no secure measures outside of the cottages.

School isn't much different in CHS as it is "on the outs" (in the outside world). Many residents, however, are dropouts, and the transition back to classes can be difficult. Guest speakers, author visits, and other special events are part of the CHS program.

THE ARTHUR G. DOZIER SCHOOL FOR BOYS

The Arthur G. Dozier School for Boys was a reform school in a small town in northwestern Florida from 1900 to 2011. It was one of the largest juvenile reform institutions in the country. Throughout its history, allegations of abuse, beatings, torture, and even murder surfaced. Former residents who are still living have recounted horrifying examples of brutal mistreatment at the school that many refer to as hell.

John Bonner sits on a bed frame in the now abandoned cottage where he lived at the Dozier School for Boys. Testimony from former residents such as Bonner led investigators to pursue allegations of severe brutality and slave labor at the school, which operated until 2011.

The institution, like many in the South, practiced segregation, keeping white and black students apart. Some evidence suggests the black students were treated much more harshly than white students. While segregation ended in 1964, the cruel treatment of youth did not. In 1968, after a visit to the school, Florida governor Claude Kirk Jr. said, "Somebody should have blown the whistle [on this school] a long time ago." Yet physical abuse, such as hog-tying students and placing them in leg chains, along with extensive time in solitary confinement, continued for decades.

Finally, the allegations were confirmed by investigations by the Florida Department of Law Enforcement in 2010 and the US Department of Justice in 2011. The findings forced the school to close. In 2013 a team of forensic anthropologists—scientists who work to determine the age, race, sex, and other aspects of skeletal remains—began exhuming (digging up) bodies of youth who had died during their stay at the school and been buried in unmarked graves on school property. At least ninety-eight people died at the school over the years—two staff members and ninety-six boys between the ages of six and eighteen. The initial digs found fifty bodies. While some appear to have died natural deaths, questions—bolstered by testimony of former residents who are still living—remain about the cause of death of the others. While scientists may be able to shed more light on a brutal chapter in reform school history, the full story of what happened at the Dozier school may never be known.

For more than a decade, residents published their poetry in *Diverse-City*, a magazine published by the Hennepin County Library. In addition to grades, CHS uses a system of positives and negatives to motivate students to behave. Positives create more privileges.

Residents stay at CHS for three to six months, to receive therapy. The Girls' Focus Program and the Juvenile Sex Offender Program offer more intensive therapy. Residents in these programs often serve up to a year. The juvenile court judge decides, based on evidence, when a resident is allowed to return home. CHS staff use cognitive behavioral therapy (CBT) to teach residents skills to change their destructive and antisocial ways of thinking. In particular, residents learn to practice responsibility, and to develop respect, empathy, and safe and healthy relationships. Residents also may participate in programs to deal with issues such as addiction.

> "MOST KIDS SHOULD BE GIVEN A SECOND CHANCE AND AN OPPORTUNITY TO START OVER WHILE THEY ARE STILL YOUNG. THEY DON'T EVEN KNOW WHO THEY ARE. THEY CAN BE REHABILITATED, BUT NOT WITH YEARS AND YEARS IN PRISON."
>
> —JORDAN, SENTENCED TO TWENTY YEARS IN PRISON FOR A CRIME COMMITTED AT FIFTEEN

While at CHS, residents can read books, watch videos, and play computer games. Access to entertainment hinges on participating in therapy, following the rules of the cottage, and behaving in school. Family visiting hours are more frequent than in juvenile detention centers, and CHS hosts twice annual family nights where families can visit with residents, meet their teachers, and share a meal on tables set up in the gym.

BOOT CAMPS

Boot camps are a type of reform school. The nation's first juvenile boot camp began operation in Orleans Parish, Louisiana, in 1985.

COGNITIVE BEHAVIORAL THERAPY

Research has shown that push-ups, digging holes, and other physical training and punishments aren't approaches that motivate offenders to change their thinking and their behavior. In fact, programs based on punishment and deterrence appear to actually increase criminal recidivism. On the other hand, research shows that therapeutic approaches based on counseling and skill building are better at reducing recidivism, even among the highest risk offenders. In particular, mental training, in the form of cognitive behavioral therapy, is one of the most successful treatments for youth offenders in reform school settings. This treatment is a problem-focused approach to help people identify the beliefs, thoughts, and behaviors that caused them to commit crimes. By focusing on causes, youth offenders can more successfully change their way of thinking and behaving.

As a teen, Louis Rivera participated in the moral therapy program, an experimental treatment program at Rikers Island juvenile detention facility in New York. Of the program, which was paid for by private monies, Rivera says, "It is a steppingstone to realize what you did wrong, who you have hurt, what you can change."

By 1995 state and local agencies around the country were operating boot camps. By 2000, as evidence-based approaches took over juvenile justice, nearly one-third of state prison boot camps had closed. A survey in 2009 found only eleven states still operating boot camps for juvenile delinquents.

In many ways, boot camps are throwbacks to the harsher days of juvenile justice, where the focus was on punishment and coercion, not long-lasting positive change. Juvenile boot camps (also called shock or intensive incarceration programs) are short-term residential programs that resemble military basic training camps. One goal of the camps is to reduce recidivism. To do so, corrections staff work with residents to change their antisocial behaviors. Behavior modification therapy in boot camps involves reinforcing positive behavior with rewards and punishing negative behavior by withholding rewards. Punishment takes the form of public humiliation such as insults and name-calling, increased exercise ("drop and give me twenty"), or other methods that force youth to get with the program.

Boot camps for juvenile delinquents are based on tough military training models. As get-tough policies fade across the nation, fewer than ten states operate such camps. Here, staff at a military-style boot camp for juvenile delinquents in Pennsylvania discipline a youth *(center, against the wall)* for misbehaving during a formation.

AMIN RAFIQ ABDUL-BAARI (BORN RALPH BRAZEL JR.)

Arrested at the age of sixteen for possessing a small amount of crack cocaine, Ralph Brazel Jr. received three life sentences in prison. Ralph grew up in poverty in Florida, living first with his father and then with his grandmother. Like many youth in poverty, he found his way, along with other members of his family, into the drug trade. It seemed to him to offer opportunity for success and belonging that he found nowhere else in his community. "I didn't make a lot of money—never saw a thousand dollars—but I was living every day like it was a Friday," he said.

In prison he seized opportunities to better himself, starting with earning his GED. He learned other languages, earned various occupational certificates, and converted to Islam. Known now as Amin Rafiq Abdul-Baari, he works with incarcerated Muslim youth in prison and upon release. After serving twenty-five years, Abdul-Baari came out of prison with a clear goal of wanting to set a better example for the youth than was set for him.

In general, the boot camp model of training and discipline, for both adults and youth, is a mix of military drills with strict discipline (like the US Army's boot camp training), rehabilitation, and education. Most residents dress, talk, and exercise in the same way they would in military training. Participants follow a demanding daily schedule similar to that of a military boot camp, including rigorous drills and ceremonial rituals, intense manual labor, and demanding physical training. Residents get up early every day and have limited free time. Strict rules regulate all aspects of behavior and appearance.

Boot camps demonstrated the theory of getting tough, yet they failed in practice. Research found that the camps did not reduce recidivism regardless of whether they were for adults or juveniles.

Boot camp programs that followed a military model as well as later boot camp programs that put more emphasis on treatment also failed to reduce reoffending. Most of the research showed that boot camps worked with offenders for too brief a period (90 to 120 days) to truly modify behavior. Fear-based tactics and other forms of coercion tend not to work, especially among youth who recognize the short-term nature of such methods. Lastly, most boot camps provided little aftercare to prepare youth for life outside the camps.

CHAPTER 5

Imprisoned

A ncient Roman philosopher Cicero famously wrote, "Let the punishment be equal with the offence," which introduced the concept of proportionality in the law. Centuries later, English jurist William Blackstone noted that because of the impetuous nature of youth, the "vicious will" to commit heinous acts is often lacking. If a criminal doesn't know right from wrong, Blackstone reasoned, they are not really responsible for their crimes. The age of a criminal in relation to how that criminal should be treated, coupled with the extent of the crime, has long been a central issue in criminal law.

The American application of these ideas to youth offenders has shifted dramatically over the centuries. The get-tough policies of the mid-1990s, for example, led to more arrests, longer periods of incarceration, fewer opportunities for rehabilitation, and more youth tried and sentenced as adults. The policies also shifted the focus of juvenile justice from rehabilitation to punishment through warehousing. More young people were sentenced to time in prison than were sent to reform school. Large numbers of cases were waived from juvenile to adult criminal courts. There, automatic sentencing guidelines gave judges and juries no flexibility. The guidelines forced sentences that pushed more youth behind prison bars. This led to an increasing number of youth offenders receiving harsh sentences.

ADULT TIME FOR ADULT CRIMES

In the 1990s, all but ten states adopted or modified laws to make it easier to waive a case out of juvenile court and instead prosecute youth in adult criminal courts. Nearly half the states added crimes to the list of excluded offenses. This group of crimes includes those that law systems can shift out of juvenile court because they are either very minor (traffic violations) or because they are very serious. Crimes considered serious enough to exclude from juvenile court and transfer to adult court included murder, aggravated assault, and armed robbery. They also included nonviolent offenses such as breaking certain drug laws.

In addition, states began to lower the age at which a youth offender could go to criminal court. In Missouri, for example, youth offenders as young as twelve could go to criminal court for any felony. In all but two states—Nebraska and New York—a juvenile court judge was allowed to transfer youth at certain age limits to adult court for crimes such as property, drug, and public disorder offenses. Thirteen states added or modified laws to provide for a mandatory minimum period of incarceration before parole would be considered for serious and violent crimes. While some of these laws have since been appealed and overturned, the original intent was to ensure that youth did hard time for most crimes, even nonviolent offenses. As a result, the number of offenders under the age of eighteen who were admitted to state prisons more than doubled from thirty-four hundred in 1985 to seventy-four hundred in 1997.

LIFE IN PRISON

Youth offenders who have been sentenced for serious crimes are likely to go to a juvenile prison. Most of these are state run, although many are run by for-profit private companies. One such prison is the Pendleton Juvenile Correctional Facility in Pendleton, Indiana. This maximum security prison houses youth who are any of the following: high-risk, assaultive, sexual offenders, persons with serious mental health disorders, and who are at risk of escaping. Like the routine at other juvenile facilities, life at Pendleton involves drab uniforms and rote tasks. But because the offenders are dangerous, the guards are equipped with riot gear: batons, helmets, and cuffs. One guard at the facility said that "this generation of juveniles are a lot more reckless. They are probably ten times more reckless than an adult offender."

One way prisons work to manage high-risk inmates is through a future soldier program that prepares offenders to serve in the military. But not all offenders focus on their future. Many are at risk of harming themselves. Violence among offenders is a threat too. So Pendleton offers a wide variety of therapeutic programs. Other programs focus on violence prevention, learning job skills, and preparing for life after release. The result for some inmates is positive. One offender said, "[Through the programs] I actually wanted to change my life. Before I was just going to do my time. Get out and do the same thing I did. But now, I want to go back to doing good."

KIDS FOR CASH

Many prisons in the United States are run by state and local governments and are nonprofits. However, some are run by private companies to earn a profit. Sometimes, the for-profit approach has led to unethical, illegal behavior. For example, in 2008, two judges in Wilkes-Barre, Pennsylvania, were accused of accepting bribes from Robert Mericle, a real-estate developer who owned two private, for-profit correctional facilities. In return for almost $3 million, judges Mark Ciavarella and Michael Conahan sentenced youth offenders to Mericle's facilities, often for very minor offenses and for the maximum allowed time.

In 2011 both judges were convicted on multiple counts of illegal behavior. For their crimes, Ciavarella was sentenced to twenty-eight years and Conahan to seventeen and one-half years in federal prison. Mericle was later sentenced to one year in federal prison for bribery. He also settled a $17.75 million lawsuit brought on behalf of offenders who had appeared before Ciavarella.

Some states contract with private companies to operate prisons. Yet they are not always run well. For example, complaints of abuse and neglect are common at the privately run East Mississippi Correctional Facility in Jackson. Christopher Lindsey *(right)*, a former inmate at the facility, lost his sight as a result of months of medical neglect. He has glaucoma, which went untreated at the facility.

THE HARSH REALITIES OF ADULT PRISON

But not all youth serve out their sentences in juvenile prison. Those who turn eighteen (older in some states) and who still have time left to serve are headed to adult prison. Youth in adult facilities are at much greater risk of harm than if they are housed in juvenile facilities. The suicide rate for youth in adult prisons, for example, is five times the rate in the general youth population and eight times the rate in juvenile detention facilities. Youth in adult facilities are also more likely to be violently victimized. A study from 1998 showed that sexual assault was five times more likely, beatings by staff nearly twice as likely, and attacks with weapons almost 50 percent more common for youth who are locked up in adult facilities.

Various recent studies have found that the recidivism rate for young people who served time in adult prisons is significantly higher than for those who remained in the juvenile system. Research from the Centers for Disease Control and Prevention (CDC), a public health US government agency, concluded that "transferring juveniles to the adult justice system is counterproductive as a strategy for deterring subsequent violence."

DEATH ROW

Young people behind bars often have their childhoods stolen by trauma, poverty, and the brutal realities of incarceration. After serving their sentences, many are released and try to rebuild their lives. Yet some have never even had that chance. These are the youth offenders who were sentenced to death for their crimes.

The death penalty has a long controversial history in the United States. In 1642 Thomas Graunger (or Granger) became the first youth known to be executed in America. Since then almost four hundred Americans have been executed for crimes committed when they were minors. The youngest—George Stinney Jr.—was executed at the age of fourteen for two murders that many people believed he had not committed and for which there was no physical evidence.

STATES WITH THE DEATH PENALTY

States that have the death penalty as of 2016

This map shows the states that currently have the death penalty and those that do not.

Since 1973 judges or juries have imposed more than one hundred death sentences on youth, about two-thirds of them on seventeen-year-olds and nearly one-third on fifteen- and sixteen-year-olds. All were prisoners on death row, for periods ranging from a few months to more than twenty years. Several inmates spent more than half their lives on death row. Of these sentences, twenty-two were carried out, beginning with the 1985 execution of Charles Rumbaugh in Texas. He was executed at the age of twenty-eight for a crime he committed when he was seventeen. More than half of these executions were in Texas, with more than half of all executions carried out against youth of color.

GEORGE STINNEY JR.

A fourteen-year-old black teen, George Stinney Jr., was arrested and tried for bludgeoning to death two young white girls, ages eleven and eight, in March 1944 in South Carolina. The hasty trial, based on circumstantial (secondhand) evidence, lasted only two hours. George had a court-appointed lawyer who did nothing to defend him. For example, he did not challenge the lack of physical evidence connecting George to the crime nor did he point out that no written record of the confession George was said to have provided had been produced. The all-white male jury deliberated only ten minutes, finding George guilty and sentencing him to death by electric chair. With this sentence, George became the youngest person ever executed in the United States in the twentieth century.

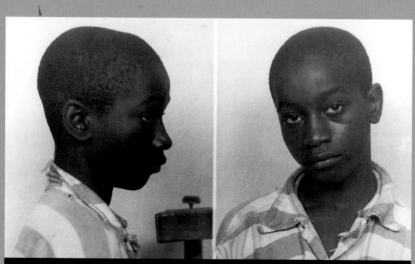

Fourteen-year-old George Stinney Jr. posed for a mugshot in 1944. He was executed that same year for a murder conviction that was overturned in 2014.

Unlike modern death row convictions, for which appeals may be filed to a higher court, George's was not. He was executed in June 1944, less than ninety days after the original crime took place. Because of his small size—just 5 feet 1 (1.6 meters) and weighing less than 100 pounds (45 kilograms)—George had to sit on a phone book in the large electric chair. The electrode proved too big for his leg, and the straps did not fit around his slender body. As the lethal electricity flowed through his body, the mask slipped from his face, exposing his tear-filled eyes. A 1991 television movie, *Carolina Skeletons*, shows the horror of the execution.

Evidence connecting George to the crime for which he was executed was slim at best, and many observers felt he did not receive a fair trial. So members of his family and civil rights organizations fought for years to clear his name. They finally succeeded when an appeal went before South Carolina judge Carmen Tevis Mullen in January 2014. Mullen's December 2014 decision, a court order, reviews the facts of the case from 1944. It also reviews new testimony and statements from surviving family members and witnesses, as well as scientific evidence. Mullen outlines various constitutional violations in George's case, many directly related to his age and his inability to participate in his own defense. In conclusion, Mullen writes, "I can think of no greater injustice. . . . I find by a preponderance of evidence standard, that a violation of the Defendant's procedural due process rights tainted his prosecution. . . . I hereby vacate [overturn] the Defendant's conviction." In 2014 Stinney would have been eighty-four years old.

> **"I CAN THINK OF NO GREATER INJUSTICE. . . . I FIND BY A PREPONDERANCE OF EVIDENCE STANDARD, THAT A VIOLATION OF THE DEFENDANT'S PROCEDURAL DUE PROCESS RIGHTS TAINTED HIS PROSECUTION. . . . I HEREBY VACATE [OVERTURN] THE DEFENDANT'S CONVICTION."**
>
> —JUDGE CARMEN TEVIS MULLEN, 2014

THE EIGHTH AMENDMENT TO THE US CONSTITUTION

The Eighth Amendment was adopted in 1791 as part of the Bill of Rights. The amendment says,

> *Excessive bail shall not be required, nor excessive fines imposed, nor cruel and unusual punishments inflicted.*

Cruel and unusual punishment is forbidden by the Eighth Amendment to the US Constitution. Between 1983 and 1986, five requests came before the US Supreme Court to consider whether imposing the death penalty upon a youth is a form of cruel and unusual punishment. The court rejected all five requests. With the 1987 case *Thompson v. Oklahoma*, the court finally agreed to weigh in. The court concluded in 1988 that fifteen-year-old William Wayne Thompson's death sentence for the brutal 1983 murder of his sister's former husband was unconstitutional. In the court's 5–3 decision, four of the participating eight justices agreed that executing a fifteen-year-old was cruel and unusual punishment under all circumstances. (The ninth justice, Anthony Kennedy, did not participate in the decision. Justice Sandra Day O'Connor concurred, or agreed, with the decision to vacate—or void—Thompson's death sentence but for different reasons.) In his written opinion, Justice John Paul Stevens looked at several factors. For example, he pointed to the "evolving standards of decency" argument. This legal philosophy suggests that as a society progresses, its standards of punishment must also mature to reflect current thinking among scholars, the American public, and the legal community. Stevens also said that many states, as well as other countries, had no death penalty for persons under the age of sixteen. Yet even those states that allowed it rarely used it. Stevens wrote, "Statistics . . . [lead] to the unambiguous conclusion that the imposition of the death penalty on a 15-year-old offender is now generally abhorrent to the conscience of the community." His final argument, which would play a large role in later cases, harkens back to Blackstone's concept of "vicious will." Legal tradition, Stevens said, "endorsed the proposition that less culpability should attach to a crime committed by a juvenile than to a comparable crime committed by an adult, since inexperience, less education, and less intelligence make the teenager less able to evaluate the consequences of his or her conduct, while at the same time he or she is much more apt to be motivated by mere emotion or peer pressure than is an adult."

Yet, the next year in 1989, the court upheld capital punishment against children in *Stanford v. Kentucky* and *Wilkins v. Missouri*. In those two consolidated cases, the court ruled that the Constitution does not prohibit the death penalty for capital crimes such as murder committed at the age of sixteen or seventeen. Writing for the majority in *Stanford*, Justice Antonin Scalia rejected all arguments against imposing the death penalty on minors, suggesting that broad national support for such a ban did not exist.

In 2002 Justice Stevens relied heavily on the legal concept of evolving standards of decency to write the ruling opinion in *Atkins v. Virginia*. This case involved a "mildly mentally retarded" adult man who had been convicted of murder in 1996. Although it did not deal directly with capital punishment for crimes committed by youth, the reasoning behind the court's decision laid a foundation for shifting away from imposing the death penalty on youth. In *Atkins* the court ruled that standards had shifted to accept that execution of the mentally retarded was cruel and unusual punishment and, therefore, unconstitutional. It was wrong, the court reasoned, to inflict the most severe punishment on those who may not understand the full consequences of their actions.

Paula Cooper *(in her 1985 booking photo)* pleaded guilty to the 1985 murder of Ruth Pelke, an elderly Bible school teacher, in Gary, Indiana. The next year, at sixteen years of age, Cooper was sentenced to death, becoming Indiana's youngest death row prisoner. In 1989 the Indiana Supreme Court spared Cooper's life, citing a recent state law and a US Supreme Court decision (the consolidated case of *Stanford v. Kentucky* and *Wilkins v. Missouri*) that barred executions of juveniles under the age of sixteen. She was released from prison in 2013 and committed suicide two years later.

With that background, in the 2005 *Roper v. Simmons* case, the court overruled prior decisions upholding death penalty sentences on offenders younger than eighteen. *Roper* overturned statutes (laws) in twenty-five states that had set the age lower. Writing for the majority in *Roper*, Justice Anthony Kennedy—who had joined Scalia in the *Stanford* case—cited research that found a lack of maturity and sense of responsibility in youth compared to adults. Adolescents were overrepresented statistically in almost every category of reckless behavior. Kennedy also said that almost every state recognized youthful immaturity and irresponsibility by prohibiting people under the age of eighteen from voting, serving on juries, and marrying without parental consent. Further, Kennedy said that states were increasingly unwilling to apply capital punishment to youth offenders. At that time, twenty states had the juvenile death penalty on the books, but only six had executed prisoners for crimes committed since 1989 (after the *Thompson* case). Only three had done so in the previous ten years, and the five states that had allowed the juvenile death penalty in 1989 had outlawed it by 2005.

The court also looked at practices in other countries to support the ruling. Kennedy noted that only seven countries other than the United States—Iran, Pakistan, Saudi Arabia, Yemen, Nigeria, the Democratic Republic of the Congo, and China—had executed juvenile offenders. By the time *Roper* was heard, all other countries had either abolished the death penalty for juveniles or publicly rejected it. Kennedy wrote that "capital punishment must be limited to those offenders who commit 'a narrow category of the most serious crimes' and whose extreme culpability makes them 'the most deserving of execution' . . . juvenile offenders cannot with reliability be classified among the worst offenders." Since capital punishment is reserved for only the worst offenders, Kennedy reasoned that juveniles should never be subject to the death penalty.

LIFE WITHOUT HOPE

For years, however, the overwhelming majority of states allowed life without parole for offenders younger than sixteen. Some states made the sentence mandatory for defendants convicted in criminal court of certain violent offenses. In Kansas and Vermont, for example, ten-year-olds were eligible for life without parole if the crime was particularly violent. In Washington State, eight-year-olds could be sent to prison for life without parole. Most of these laws were passed during the get-tough years. Yet as cases such as Sara Kruzan's became publicized, many Americans voiced doubts on this approach. (In 1995 seventeen-year-old Kruzan, a victim of sexual trafficking, was convicted of murdering her abusive pimp and was sentenced to life in prison without parole.)

SARA KRUZAN

Unlike many other youthful offenders, Sara didn't struggle at school. She was, she said, an "over achiever" who ran for student body president, won awards, and participated in high school sports in her hometown of Riverside, California. Yet unknown to her friends, her life outside of school had a completely different face. Recruited at the age of eleven by a thirty-one-year-old pimp, or sex trafficker, named George Gilbert (G. G.) Howard, Sara at first saw the man as a father figure. (Her own father was in prison. She would only meet him three times in her childhood.) Howard bought gifts for Sara and gave her advice, so she believed he was someone who cared for her. But Howard raped Sara when she was just thirteen. He then forced her to work for him as a prostitute. Howard sold Sara and other young girls for sex, seven days a week, twelve hours a night. For three years, the abuse continued until a rival pimp gave Sara a horrific choice: either kill Howard or the rival pimp would kill Sara's mother. In 1994 Sara shot Howard dead.

OF HER SENTENCING IN 1995, SARA RECALLED, "MY JUDGE TOLD ME THAT I LACKED MORAL SCRUPLES." OF BEING SENTENCED TO LIFE WITHOUT PAROLE, SHE SAYS SHE KNEW IT MEANT "I'M GONNA DIE HERE."

Sara, aged seventeen, was tried as an adult for the murder. At her trial, her lawyers argued for a less harsh sentence because the circumstances in Sara's life as a victim of sex trafficking under Howard had been brutal. Yet, the jury of seven women and five men found her guilty of first-degree murder. In May 1995, Sara's judge sentenced her to life without parole. While incarcerated, friends and juvenile justice reform organizations launched a social media movement to earn her release. The movement gathered support, and in 2013, after nineteen years in prison, Kruzan was released.

Many people felt it was not right to sentence minors—who are not legally able to drive—to prison for life without the chance to rehabilitate and live outside of prison walls.

This changed in 2010 with the *Graham v. Florida* decision. Building off the logic of *Roper v. Simmons*, the Supreme Court held that youth cannot be sentenced to life imprisonment without parole for non-homicide offenses. Kennedy's majority opinion reasoned that it was cruel and unusual punishment to impose a life sentence that would provide no realistic opportunity for a youth offender to obtain release. Kennedy wrote such a sentence "deprives the convict of the most basic liberties without giving hope of restoration. . . . As one court observed in overturning a life without parole sentence for a juvenile defendant, this sentence "means denial of hope; it means that good behavior and character improvement are immaterial; it means that whatever the future might hold in store for the mind and spirit of [the convict], he will remain in prison for the rest of his days." Life without hope was as cruel and unusual a punishment as death.

"IF YOU LOCK PEOPLE UP AND DON'T TEACH THEM SOMETHING, IT'S A LOSE/LOSE SITUATION."
—TRAVIS, SEVENTEEN

In the 2012 case *Miller v. Alabama*, the court went further, deciding that mandatory sentences of life without the possibility of parole were unconstitutional for youth offenders for any crime. Justice Elena Kagan wrote for the majority, saying, "Mandatory life without parole for a juvenile [prevents] consideration of his chronological age and its hallmark features—among them immaturity, impetuosity, and failure to appreciate risks and consequences."

In late 2014, the Supreme Court agreed to hear *Toca v. Louisiana*, a case meant to clarify whether the *Miller v. Alabama* decision should be applied retroactively. A retroactive decision in *Toca* would have allowed thousands of individuals serving mandatory life-without-parole sentences for crimes committed as youth an opportunity for

MARK

Mark, like many youthful offenders, asks the juvenile justice system, "Why should I walk around with a label on me because I made a mistake when I was young? Can I get a second chance in life?" Sentenced to thirteen years, Mark describes the boredom of life inside. About a typical day, Mark says, "Wake up, wash up. Same thing, different day." From his experience in the juvenile system, Mark notes that the only practical effect of locking young kids away is that it "makes [them] a better criminal."

resentencing and a second chance at a new life. The court, after agreeing to take the case and hear the oral argument, decided not to hear the case, leaving each state to sort out how to apply the *Miller* case.

THE OTHER DEATH PENALTY

The US Supreme Court ruled in *Roper* that juveniles could not be sentenced to the death penalty. But many juveniles in the United States face another kind of lethal violence at the hands of state authorities: being shot dead on the street by a police officer. High-profile shootings of young civilians by the police in 2014 and 2015 thrust this issue into the public arena. The Black Lives Matter movement was at the forefront of the protest movement. According to data collected by the CDC, 7 percent of people killed by law enforcement agents are teenagers. And the number of people killed by law enforcement shows disproportionate minority contact. One report found that Native Americans are the most likely to be killed by law enforcement, followed by African Americans, Latinos, whites, and Asian Americans. African Americans, who make up 13 percent of the US population, are victims in 26 percent of police shootings. They are killed at 2.8 times the rate of white non-Latinos

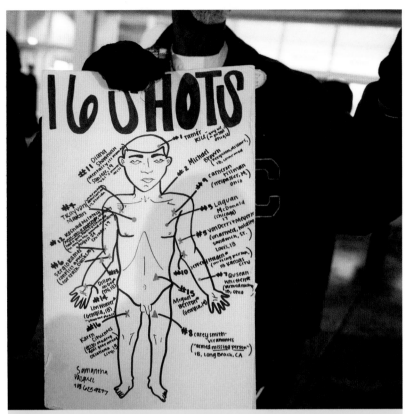

In December 2015, demonstrators protest in front of police headquarters in Chicago, Illinois, over the fatal 2014 shooting of Laquan McDonald—a seventeen-year-old black male. Police officer Jason Van Dyke shot the teen sixteen times. In response to mounting pressure, Chicago's mayor, Rahm Emanuel, fired Chicago police superintendant Garry McCarthy in 2015. McCarthy, Emanuel, and Cook County state's attorney Anita Alvarez have been accused of trying to cover up the shooting.

and 4.3 times the rate of Asians. Latinos are victimized by police killings at almost twice the rate of white non-Latinos. While police shootings have fallen greatly since the 1960s, a young black male just out of his teen years (between the ages of twenty and twenty-four) is still the most likely to be shot by a police officer.

CHAPTER 6

ALTERNATIVES

Placing youthful offenders in alternative programs rather than in secure detention facilities has led to less crime on the streets and less government spending on offenders. Much of this is a result of the Juvenile Detention Alternatives Initiative, which has reduced the number of young people locked up on an average day by 43 percent. Yearly admissions to detention have decreased 39 percent. More than half the reduction in admissions is among youth of color, who are overrepresented in secure detention. A *New York Times* editorial in 2009 noted that "communities that have been most faithful to the new [JDAI] model have registered the most impressive results, with some districts locking up only about a quarter of the number of youngsters as before. These efforts show that it is possible to treat children humanely without compromising public safety and deserve to be replicated nationwide."

NOT SCARED STRAIGHT

JDAI programs are evidence-based—research and data demonstrate they are effective. But not all reform programs in the history of the juvenile justice world—even some of the most popular approaches— have been able to prove that they work. One such popular program was the Scared Straight approach of the 1970s. It was launched with inmates serving life sentences at a New Jersey prison. Kids in the Scared Straight program were delinquent or at-risk youth. They would visit the prison, where inmates would scream threats and obscenities at them. The inmates would then discuss life in adult prisons, including stories of rape and murder. The idea behind the program was that fear would change the behavior of delinquent youth and convince them to go straight. The program received favorable media attention and was soon launched in more than thirty jurisdictions around the country.

"COMMUNITIES THAT HAVE BEEN MOST FAITHFUL TO THE NEW [JDAI] MODEL HAVE REGISTERED THE MOST IMPRESSIVE RESULTS, WITH SOME DISTRICTS LOCKING UP ONLY ABOUT A QUARTER OF THE NUMBER OF YOUNGSTERS AS BEFORE. THESE EFFORTS SHOW THAT IT IS POSSIBLE TO TREAT CHILDREN HUMANELY WITHOUT COMPROMISING PUBLIC SAFETY AND DESERVE TO BE REPLICATED NATIONWIDE."
—*NEW YORK TIMES* EDITORIAL, 2009

In 1999 a documentary called *Scared Straight: 20 Years Later* was shown on US television. The filmmakers claimed that ten of the twelve juveniles attending the program remained offense-free at the three-month follow-up. In 2011 a new TV show, *Beyond Scared Straight*, began airing on the A&E network. The episodes focused on a group of at-risk youth who participated in prison-based intervention programs. The show claimed similar success with kids who had participated in the updated program. Yet, when researchers, not the film producers, began digging into the data, they found quite different results.

Research looking at data over a twenty-five-year period in eight different jurisdictions found that fear-based programs are not effective as a crime prevention strategy. In fact, the research showed an increase in criminality in the experimental group when compared to a no-treatment control group. So doing nothing would have been better than exposing juveniles to the harsh, confrontational programs.

ALTERNATIVE PROGRAMS

Many successful alternative programs for youth offenders involve allowing individuals to stay in their own homes and schools. They must follow severe restrictions, which limit their freedom and choices. Some programs place youth in shelters or other out-of-home placements, while some may require youth to mow grass in local parks and perform other community services. Some of these programs are pre-adjudication—the youth agrees to go into the program instead of having a judge hear the case. Others are post-adjudication—the judge orders an offender into a program such as community service. Some are short-term programs, while others might last for a year. None locks a young person behind bars.

All alternatives are evidence-based practices that are proven to reduce recidivism. Alternatives are designed for time-limited rather than long-term treatment. Long stays lead to a greater likelihood that youth will violate program rules and end up in secure detention. Long stays also mean that fewer spots are available for other kids, forcing the system to hold eligible juveniles in secure detention.

The alternative to the detention movement has proven successful for many reasons on many levels. In general, 20 percent of youth offenders are good kids who make a one-time bad decision, face their penalty, and move on to a normal life, if their journey into the justice system didn't cause them harm. Another 20 percent lead a life of crime because the odds are so stacked against them that they cannot escape poverty, broken families, drugs, gangs, and other negative influences. The 60 percent in the middle—the majority of kids who offend—benefit from the reform movement. Before JDAI these offending youth would be locked up and would suffer all the negative consequences. Now, they are diverted into alternative programs. The evidence is clear that by using alternatives to putting kids behind cell bars, youth and society are both better served.

COMMUNITY SERVICE

The juvenile justice system of the twenty-first century has a range of alternative programs for youth offenders. Among the most common alternatives to detention is community service. Community service is typically for low-risk offenses such as truancy and vandalism. Sometimes called "sentenced to serve," this alternative was built off the idea of restorative justice from the 1970s. In this model, offenders are understood to have hurt their community. Their punishment is to help heal it or at least to help clean it up. Teens who perform community service may mow lawns, pick up trash, or work within a library. Community service is intentional and youth-focused. For example, JDAI treats community service not as punishment but as a way to build skills among youth and to help them have a meaningful, positive experience in life.

JUVENILE JUSTICE REFORM ALTERNATIVES ARE EVIDENCE-BASED PRACTICES THAT ARE PROVEN TO REDUCE RECIDIVISM.

HOME CONFINEMENT

Home confinement, or house arrest, is a community-based program that allows offenders to live at home while attending school or work or both. They follow a strict schedule and are closely monitored electronically by wearing ankle bracelets that send location information back to the juvenile probation staff. Sometimes, juvenile probation officers frequently contact youth under house arrest in person or by phone or both. Youth demonstrate their desire to behave responsibly by promising to follow the judge's order and not violate their probation by

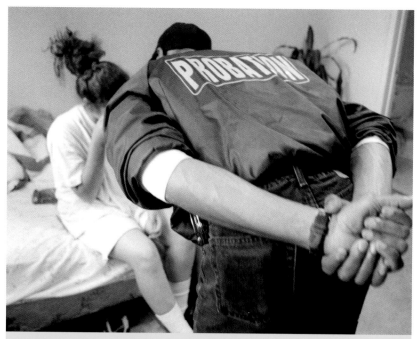

A probation officer makes a surprise visit to a juvenile girl on home confinement. Probation officers can make a positive impact on the lives of juvenile offenders by checking in on them frequently to make sure they are working their plan.

"breaking the bracelet" (removing the device). This might help persuade the judge to hand down a lighter sentence or none at all.

One of the keys to the high success rate of home confinement is a probation officer's frequent, random, and unannounced supervision visits. This minimizes the chances that youth will commit crimes and maximizes the chance they'll appear in court when scheduled. Small caseloads for home detention programs ensure effective supervision as well.

JUVENILE INTENSIVE SUPERVISION PROGRAMS

JISPs are electronic home monitoring on steroids. Judges place youth offenders who are at higher risk for reoffending into these programs. They remain under house arrest but have a much higher level of contact with their probation officers than do low-risk offenders.

RECONCILIATION AND RESTORATIVE JUSTICE

Reconciliation and restorative justice programs are based on the simple idea that rather than the state punishing a criminal, the offender restores, or repairs, the harm that person has done to the community. The theory is based on the belief that an offender who has had to fix the hurt caused by the criminal act or who faces and apologizes to the victim or victims of that act is less likely to reoffend.

In restorative justice models, people who have been harmed by a criminal act come together to determine the best methods to fix the damage. This may be by repaying a victim or by meeting the victim. Most juvenile justice programs stress that an offender learn empathy for victims. This can happen when the victim and offender meet face-to-face in a conference session. For example, Cody Gates was arrested for aggravated battery when a firecracker-throwing prank hurt someone. Cody served three months in detention and also had to meet and talk to his victim. There, Cody told the person he had hurt that he was sorry for his action. Cody said how important it was for him that his victim and the authorities at the conference "got to hear it from me." This meeting between offender and victim is called reconciliation. It allows victims "to communicate the personal, financial, and material impact of the crime to

the offender, be recognized by the offender, and ask important questions such as Why me? or What were you trying to achieve?" This type of interpersonal communication between offender and victim is often the most critical piece of healing for both parties.

Campus supervisor Zach Mamuzich speaks to teens about a restorative justice program at the high school where he works in Colorado. These programs are designed as an alternative to suspension to keep kids in school.

JISPs also connect youth to therapeutic services. Kids in these programs typically live with substance abuse problems, difficult family issues, mental illness, or are failing at school. So youth in JISPs go to counseling, observe a curfew, and are regularly tested for drug and alcohol use. They also do supervised community service. The length of time in the program varies, but the average is one year. Youth who break the rules may end up in a residential placement or secure detention.

DAY TREATMENT PROGRAMS AND SHELTER CARE

Day (or evening) treatment programs—also called day or evening reporting centers—are a highly structured, community-based alternative that provide intensive supervision to offenders. They are used pre- and post-adjudication. Day treatment programs serve delinquent youth in nonresidential settings. They aim to help improve academic and vocational (job-based) achievement and school attendance while also reducing problem behaviors. These community programs provide six to twelve hours of daily supervision and structured activities. Youth in these programs require more intensive oversight than an in-home program can provide. Offenders are required to report to the treatment facility on a daily basis at specified times for a certain number of days each week, generally at least five. They are allowed to return home at night.

A companion alternative program is an evening reporting center. Cook County, Illinois, created a system of reporting centers that provides structure and supervision to offending youth from four in the afternoon until nine at night. This is the after-school period when most youth crime occurs. Located in high-crime neighborhoods, the centers are run by nonprofit, community-based providers with experience and expertise in dealing with neighborhood youth. The agency hires, trains, and supervises local staff, who provide intensive, individualized supervision to generally fewer than twenty youth per site.

Shelter care offers nonsecure residential care for kids who need short-term placement of one to thirty days outside the home. It's an option for youth who do not have a parent or family member to live with. These youth also need more supervision than nonresidential options can offer. Shelter care can be used both pre- and post-adjudication. Juveniles have a daily schedule of structured educational and recreational activities. These shelter care programs are a modern version of Chicago's Hull House. Staff generally supervise youth at shelter care twenty-four hours a day, seven days a week.

One such modern example is the Harkins House in Hillsboro, Oregon, just west of Portland. This short-term residential shelter care and evaluation program provides evaluation and individual care for delinquent youth placed in shelter care. The program provides recreational, artistic, and cultural activities, as well as schooling and counseling. The sites run twenty-four hours a day, seven days a week, with professional staff to care for and supervise the young residents.

GROUP HOMES AND SPECIALIZED FOSTER CARE

Group homes are community-based, long-term alternative facilities where kids live while going to school, working, or both. While they vary in size, group homes normally serve five to fifteen juveniles who are placed there through a court order. Judges send kids to group homes pre- and post-adjudication. A youth might be placed in a group home after leaving a secure placement but before returning home. This option helps kids gather support, learn responsibility, and demonstrate they can handle their newfound freedom.

Specialized foster care is a post-adjudication option that trains families to care for youth with chronic and severe delinquency. Foster-care parents provide youth with one-on-one mentoring and consistent consequences for breaking rules. Judges will typically send kids to foster care if the youth's biological family is violent or lives with substance abuse and other harmful behaviors. In a foster-care home, parents closely supervise youth, who go to school and therapy sessions. Many foster-care kids work in the community, where adults supervise them.

Lesbian social worker Naimah Johnson *(right)* is in the process of adopting her foster daughter, Ashley *(left)*, eighteen. The two met when Ashley, who identifies as queer, was in a group foster home where Johnson works. Foster-care agencies and group homes are working harder to meet the needs of lesbian; gay; bisexual; transgender; and queer/questioning (LGBTQ) professionals and teens. LGBTQ teen offenders are at a higher risk than straight juvenile offenders of rejection and abuse in their families and from the juvenile justice system.

In some ways, group and foster homes resemble reform schools, especially with the focus on therapy. Yet these placements bear little of the stigma of being locked up. They also aim to keep offenders in their communities, building a sense of belonging rather than alienation.

TREATMENT PROGRAMS

For many young people, untreated mental health and substance abuse issues lead to crime. For many of these youth, the best alternative is placement in a mental health or substance treatment facility, where trained staff work with them. Staff lead group therapy sessions and counsel youth one-on-one. Staff members work with medical professionals and human services workers to help kids get sober. Treatment also helps offenders get the medication they need so they can be sober and clearheaded when they appear for their court dates, go to school, or work at a job. Some of these placements are in treatment centers. Others are in group homes.

OUTDOOR PROGRAMS AND MENTOR PROGRAMS

For other youth, the issues that lead them to crime are based in the dangerous, urban environments in which they live. Then the best solution is often to remove offenders from their neighborhoods and the larger urban environment. Outdoor programs place urban youth in wilderness settings, where they take part in boating, hiking, and other structured outdoor activities. A cross between summer camp and boot camp, these programs seek to change behavior by changing the environment for the better. Outdoor programs also require youth to work, live, eat, and play together to achieve goals cooperatively rather than as competitors.

"I'VE BEEN THROUGH IT ALL, SO NOW I'M TRYING NOT TO GO BACK TO IT BECAUSE I'VE COME FROM IT. . . . NOW I'M STARTING FROM SCRATCH AND DOING IT MYSELF. I'M SEEING WHERE LIFE TAKES ME."
—ROBERT, SIXTEEN

Mentoring programs also help kids succeed. In Minnesota's Hennepin County, for example, programs with community coaches and juvenile court outreach workers foster relationships between caring adults and youth. The coaches work directly with youth who have been moved out of detention. Adult community coaches provide emotional support for youth that might be lacking at home. They mentor youth to link them to resources in the community that can help them meet their goals. The outreach workers help keep an offender's family involved in all aspects of the legal process. They also help make sure youth show up at

DOLPHY JORDAN

Dolphy Jordan was born to a mother who was addicted to heroin. So Dolphy was born addicted to heroin. "I came from a dysfunctional and abusive childhood," Jordan says. Child Protection Services removed him from his home. He moved from home to home, and while at school, he was in and out of trouble due to a lack of stability and adult care in his life. With trouble all around him, Dolphy fell into crime himself. At the age of sixteen, he was arrested and convicted for first-degree murder.

Sentenced to a lengthy prison term, Dolphy at first was angry and scared. But as he matured, his thoughts turned not just to his own future but to the consequences of his past actions. After twenty-one years in prison, where he focused on improving his life, Jordan became a free man. Once outside he completed a college degree in social work. He works with at-risk youth, focusing on juveniles in prison. He knows the hopelessness that can take over, but he also knows from his own story that change is possible. "I will not be defined by my worst decision," Jordan said, "I will be defined by the person I have become."

their court appearances. The consequences of missed court dates can be severe, likely resulting in placement in secure detention.

Barry Krisberg, former president of the National Council on Crime and Delinquency, says that the range of alternative programs demonstrates that "JDAI is one of the most important and successful reform movements in the history of juvenile justice. . . . JDAI created tools and a cadre [group] of experts who could assist jurisdictions with interest in reform."

CHAPTER 7

REENTERING

Each year approximately one hundred thousand youth are released from the US juvenile justice system. Some make it, others do not. For example, many kids go back to families struggling with domestic violence, substance abuse, unresolved mental health problems, and poverty. Many return to neighborhoods with few support programs, high crime rates, and poorly performing schools. Many youth also have a parent who is incarcerated or has been incarcerated at some point in the youth's life. These are the very same elements that play a major role in criminal behavior.

The transition out of the structure of confinement or alternative placement can prove to be overwhelming for many people. Many youth struggle with the lack of routine that freedom brings. They also struggle with social barriers—lack of education, poverty, and racism—that make success in the world outside of bars difficult. As one researcher noted, "Young offenders recovering from drug or alcohol abuse often have not had experience filling their time with anything but consuming drugs and being high . . . a whole new behavior pattern may have to be developed." Some kids are so unable to cope with life on the outside that they commit suicide.

In addition, a criminal record makes some parts of everyday life impossible. A criminal record may make it more difficult to get state

Reynolds Wintersmith was sentenced in 1994, when he was a teen, to life in prison for drug dealing. As part of a larger effort to pull back on the harsh sentences of earlier decades, President Barack Obama commuted the sentence in 2015. Wintersmith is now working as a counselor at a second-chance alternative school in Chicago. Among his duties at the school is to lead talking circles with students to focus on conflict resolution.

identification and other legal documents. Criminal records often remain on the public record for some time before they are sealed or closed. While the information is available to the public, employers and other people considering a youth offender for a position have access to it and may decide not to hire or accept that person because of the offender's record. Even if the records are sealed, former offenders have large gaps of time in their education, employment, or extracurricular activities that can be difficult to explain to a potential employer or school. So a criminal record may lead to lifelong barriers that reduce access to stable housing, education, and employment. All the collateral damage of incarceration can lead to the creation of second-class citizens.

AFTERCARE

To help youth offenders make the reentry into society, case workers in systems that have enough workers, time, and money put together comprehensive case management plans for each offender who is facing release. A good, detailed discharge plan includes coordination of drug rehabilitation and job training, work programs, housing, adult mentoring, and life skills training for offenders after they are released. Reentry services are often placed in neighborhoods with the highest number of released offenders to allow them to get easily to the services.

Nonprofit and faith-based organizations are strong providers of youth reentry services. Some help families who want to bring released youth into their homes. Others offer affordable housing and supportive services, such as food and transportation vouchers, for youth who cannot safely return home. In-home counseling with a released youth and the offender's family to address the root causes of delinquency has reduced recidivism by as much as 50 percent, according to one study. All these services increase a person's chances of being successful in school, on the job, and in relationships with other people.

Because youth sentences are often only a few months, caseworkers start to develop prerelease plans when youth are first placed in residential or transition programs. Most youth have plans that run for six months, with a year of follow-up. Prerelease plans are tailored to the needs of the individual, based on information from the youth offender, the family, and attorneys. Plans can be modified as needed.

One study of reentry programs concluded that if well implemented, reentry services can "improve both intermediate adjustment to the community and success in [not reoffending]." Further, the study found that youth receiving reentry services with mentoring had more success than youth who did not. Youth who received adult mentoring had far fewer positive drug tests and lower recidivism rates. For those who received mentoring yet did reoffend, the period between release and reoffense was longer than for youth who received no mentoring at all. In most cases, adult mentors were the key, connecting youth to educational, employment, and mental health services that lead to success.

While most offending youth go back into the same situations that led them to commit a crime, many leave their confinement with empowering life skills they never had. Once outside, they are able to create a new support system. Some will fail and end up reoffending. But overall, research shows that community-based reentry programs set up youth to overcome barriers and rebuild their lives in the community.

REENTRY BARRIERS

Even with a strong aftercare plan, young people still face barriers to a successful life and may have trouble resisting the temptations that led to their incarceration. Many returning youth lack skills to cope with adult responsibilities. One national study found that within twelve months of reentry to the community, 70 percent of previously incarcerated youth were jobless or were not going to school. In these cases, plans were typically not in place to help youth exiting confinement. When returning youth do not have a plan to guide them, about two-thirds will not complete their education. Lacking a solid education, many have trouble finding jobs and fall back into crime.

Yet getting back into school is sometimes challenging. Some schools view formerly incarcerated youth as too difficult to manage, and so they place obstacles to reenrollment. Often, for example, schoolwork a youth may have completed in detention does not count toward graduation credits.

"WHEN BAD THINGS HAPPEN TO YOUNG PEOPLE, THEY SOMETIMES DO BAD THINGS IN RETURN BECAUSE THEY ARE HURTING. GIVE THEM A CHANCE, GIVE THEM SOME HELP— DON'T JUST SEND THEM AWAY."

—EMMA, SEVENTEEN

THE NEW JIM CROW

Discriminatory Jim Crow laws were passed in a majority of states in the late 1880s. Slaves had been freed, and the US Constitution had new amendments to guarantee citizenship and voting rights to people in the United States, regardless of race or color. All the same, many white Americans wanted a way to maintain racial segregation.

The Jim Crow laws created legal segregation in every aspect of daily life, from schools and restaurants to bathrooms, drinking fountains, and transportation systems. Jim Crow laws remained in place until civil rights legislation in the mid-1960s outlawed racial segregation.

In her 2010 book *The New Jim Crow: Mass Incarceration in the Age of Colorblindness*, Michelle Alexander—a law professor and a civil rights advocate—equates many modern criminal sentencing trends with the Jim Crow laws of previous centuries. She cites data that shows that more black men are locked up in proportion to the overall percentage of the black population in the United States than are white men. In more than fifteen states, blacks facing drug charges are also sentenced for those charges twenty to fifty-seven times more than whites facing the same charges. Once they are released, they find many of their legal and civil rights, such as the right to vote, stripped away and any possibility for employment dramatically reduced. Alexander argues that with racial discrimination a reality of twenty-first-century life, black men and youth are facing racial segregation as persistent as that faced after the Civil War.

Alexander's book was on the *New York Times* best-seller list for more than a year. Her book and the work of advocacy groups such as the Sentencing Project helped spur the revamping of drug sentencing to be less race-biased. This led to the early release of more than sixty-six hundred inmates, many of them men of color, from federal prisons between October 30 and November 2, 2015.

And a school may view returning youth as unlikely to do well on standardized tests, which play a role in a school's overall success and in its funding. A school may therefore make it difficult for those youth to reenroll, fearing that these students will bring down a school's overall rating. Those students who are allowed to return to school often end up in alternative or charter schools that lack trained staff and other resources to help returning kids do well.

Employment is another strong predictor of criminal behavior. Research shows that individuals who are working are less likely to commit crime. Yet, when formerly incarcerated offenders seek jobs, employers may be reluctant to hire them. This is especially true if a person's criminal record has not been expunged (removed from public records), which makes it easy for an employer to do a criminal background check. Additionally, teens often lack job skills, even if they have had some vocational training while in detention, reform school, or prison. Typically, the training youth do receive is not related to what the job market actually needs.

Besides facing challenges in returning to school and the workplace, many youth who have been involved in the juvenile justice system are coping with a mix of medical, mental health, and substance abuse issues. Without a strong reentry plan to help them manage their medications and therapy, many youth quickly abandon healthy habits. They give up on their medications and therapy and fall back into old habits. In fact, research has found that recidivism often occurs just after release, sometimes within a few days. Reentry plans that help youth stay on track are critical to their ability to stay healthy—and free.

HOUSING, FINANCIAL, AND OTHER BARRIERS

Many offending youth come from poor families who live in public housing paid for by federal and local governments. The government has rules to determine who can live in this housing, and people with certain types of drug offenses do not qualify. So youth in poverty who have been incarcerated for drug offenses have trouble finding housing

Homeless youth such as nineteen-year-old Raina Young find protection from the weather anywhere they can. Here, she is hanging out at a bus terminal in New York City to keep warm.

when they are ready to reenter society. Some youth in foster care are disqualified from public housing when they reenter. When kids have no place to live, they are twice as likely as kids who have a safe place to live to end up on the streets.

According to a 2012 study in Minnesota, a high proportion of homeless youth experience health-related issues. The study found that "about one-half (52%) have a serious mental illness, with depression being the most common (29%). Sixteen percent have been told by a medical professional within the past two years that they have a drug abuse disorder (14%) or an alcohol abuse disorder (10%). Nearly one-quarter (23%) reported evidence of a traumatic brain injury." In addition, many homeless youth engage in criminal behavior, such as shoplifting, prostitution (also known as survival sex), and other behaviors to earn money to survive. Desperate, hungry, and unhealthy, homeless youth experience higher rates of recidivism than kids who have a safe place to call home.

XAVIER MCELRATH-BEY

Xavier (*pictured right, with his daughter*) grew up in poverty in Chicago in a family marked by mental illness and substance abuse. Child Protection Services removed him from his home and placed him in foster care. The foster-care family was abusive, and after years of suffering, Xavier decided that "the streets were safer" than the trauma he was enduring. He joined a gang, through which he found security and acceptance he had not known before. But

with the gang, Xavier committed various offenses and was arrested for the first time when he was only eleven years old. He was incarcerated seven times in just two years. By the time he was thirteen, he had been an accomplice to a first-degree murder. While he didn't pull the trigger, he was in the car when the murder was committed. For his role in the murder and because of his extensive juvenile record, Xavier received a sentence of twenty-five years in prison, of which he served thirteen years.

He wouldn't follow rules or behave as required in prison. So prison authorities placed him for long periods of time in solitary confinement, a small windowless cell that kept him isolated from other prisoners. In solitary he realized "how destructive and wrong I had been. I thought about all the people I had hurt." Xavier began to mature and look back on a life filled with crime, pain, and loss. He thought about his family and also about the victim of his crime. He says that focusing on his victim led him to turn around his life. He studied for and earned a college degree. After his release, he earned a master's degree in counseling and human services.

A tireless advocate for youth behind bars, McElrath-Bey has worked in the Chicago area on numerous projects related to youth justice projects, using his own story as a starting point. He dismisses the notion that youth are "born bad." He believes that circumstances such as poverty drive youth into gangs, crime, and violence. He says, "I want people to understand that kids are just kids and anyone who grows up in such circumstances can fall victim to these bad choices. I know I was once that kid and I know if I can change, they can too."

Youth coming out of detention often have financial difficulties. If they come from poor families, they may have to look to the government for Medicaid, food stamps, and other financial help. Applying for these programs is time-consuming, requiring that a person fill out forms, stand in line, or make phone calls that often require being put on hold for a long time. For many applicants, the process is also humiliating.

Reentering youth offenders may have to pay child support for any children they had when they went into placement. They may also have to pay restitution to their victims. These payments can be almost impossible to make without a decent job. To get quick cash, reentering youth can fall back into criminal behavior. Without a solid aftercare plan, many youth leaving custody find themselves in a downward spiral to incarceration, release, and rearrest.

I n the first two decades of the twenty-first century, the number of youth in the US correctional system has been at its lowest level in several decades. Much of this is due to a strong reform movement that has been very successful. Yet a certain percentage of youth offenders still do end up behind bars. What works best for those kids? Missouri has a promising answer.

THE MISSOURI MODEL

Missouri's Division of Youth Services (DYS) is the state agency responsible for taking care of delinquent youth in that state. Following a 1969 report about the chronic failure of the state's reform schools, state leadership realized a new approach was needed. Year after year, Missouri reformed all aspects of its juvenile justice system, always with the goal of smaller buildings and a less punitive approach. In 2008 DYS won an Innovations in American Government Award from the John F. Kennedy School of Government at Harvard University.

Like many state-run juvenile justice systems, DYS tried the get-tough approach and discovered it didn't work. DYS found that forcing someone to change behavior through punishment and intimidation didn't create lasting change. So instead of shaming, inflicting punishment, and isolating youth, DYS relies on therapy programs. The

As part of the Missouri Model of juvenile justice reform, teens at Hogan Street Regional Youth Center in Saint Louis, Missouri, learn restaurant job skills.

Missouri Model is built on the belief that youth are likely to engage in treatment and consider new directions only when they are in a safe, nurturing, and non-blaming environment. Trusted adults listen to and guide youth, treating them with patience, respect, and acceptance and encouraging them to try out new behaviors. The model is built upon and demonstrates one simple idea: "every young person wants to succeed—and can succeed."

The treatments take many forms. All are designed to "challenge young people and help them make lasting changes in their attitudes, beliefs, and behaviors." Through the therapy model, youth have the chance to change their lives by changing the choices they make. They can learn to let go of negative behaviors and influences and set positive goals.

While this is true of most therapy models in juvenile justice,

A teen resident of Echo Glen Children's Center, a juvenile rehabilitation facility in Snoqualmie, Washington, kisses and hugs the dog she has trained.

DYS goes a step further. It identifies the barriers to change and finds solutions to overcome them. For example, DYS has found that kids do best when they know that staff care about their success and expect them to reach their goals. So in Missouri, youth do therapeutic work in small groups, where they build safe and positive peer relationships. On the outside, peer relationships had often led to risk-taking and criminal behavior. In the therapy context, youth offenders support one another in positive ways. As their way of thinking changes, their behaviors also transform for the better.

While many juvenile justice systems are focused on the here and now, the Missouri Model recognizes that some youth lapse into serious and chronic delinquency as a way of dealing with past abuse, neglect, or trauma. Until those core issues are addressed, no real change in behavior is possible. For other youth, criminal behavior isn't rooted as deeply but is a consequence of adolescence and negative peer influence. In either case, the focus on making better decisions comes through therapy and by building relationships with caring peers and adults.

SUCCESS STORY

One key to change in Missouri was getting rid of large, prisonlike facilities and placing youth offenders in smaller buildings across the state, nearer the offenders' homes. In the small facilities, therapy programs were more successful. Missouri began this shift in juvenile justice reform while most other states were still detaining most youth who had committed criminal acts.

Another key to the Missouri Model focuses on the future and on family as a way to reduce recidivism. Missouri helps youth by reaching out to family members, to involve them as partners in treatment and aftercare. The aftercare program includes monitoring and mentoring in the first weeks following release. It also helps kids reenroll in school, get jobs, and find after-school programs.

The Missouri Model is very successful for many reasons. In part, it works because it is evidence-based, with data to support the success. For example, 90 percent of youth who live in DYS facilities earn high school credits. And because of the emphasis on aftercare, inmates don't return to the streets. They return to their communities as students. The majority of youth exiting DYS custody in 2008 (close to 90 percent) go on to high school, college, a job, or a job and school. And as of 2014, not a single youth in DYS custody has committed suicide, a risk that many youth face as they leave detention to reenter their communities.

The Missouri Model has also shown that in the short term, fewer youth locked up costs less. Missouri officials note that "steering just one high-risk delinquent teen away from a life of crime saves society $3 million to $6 million in reduced victim costs and criminal justice expenses." If youth can emerge from juvenile justice as productive citizens, they contribute to society rather than taking from it. Less funding is needed across the board for welfare, treatment, unemployment, mental health, foster care, and other systems. This means that "lives [can be] rescued, tax dollars saved, and crimes averted."

BURN IT DOWN

While many juvenile justice reformers are pleased with the changes in Missouri and other states, not everyone is applauding. Nell Bernstein, a writer and an advocate for youth in the criminal justice system, has a match in her hand instead. She believes too many youth are placed in facilities where they are treated like animals. In her 2014 book *Burning Down the House: The End of Juvenile Prison*, Bernstein argues against imprisoning youth at all. She believes that isolating youth in facilities that are focused on control and punishment denies youth the key to rehabilitation: positive relationships with caring

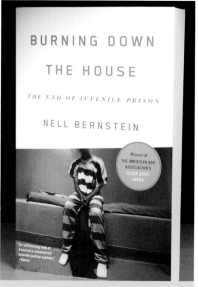

In Nell Bernstein's book *Burning Down the House*, she argues that the US juvenile justice system, particularly incarceration, does not benefit society. She recommends doing away with youth incarceration altogether.

adults. While noting successes such as the Missouri Model, Bernstein argues that the juvenile justice system in the United States is so "ineffective, racially biased and fundamentally unjust" that reform isn't enough. Incarceration of youth needs to be eliminated.

Bernstein is especially appalled by the disproportionate level of minorities in the juvenile justice system. She notes that "eighty to ninety percent of all American teenagers in confidential interviews will acknowledge that they have committed an offense or offenses that under the law they could be locked up for." But because of disproportionate minority contact, kids of color get arrested and incarcerated at much higher rates than white youth. This means that "the likelihood that they will go on to be re-incarcerated and become adult prisoners is doubled." *Burning Down the House* argues that

DARE

The primary goal of Drug Abuse Resistance Education (DARE) is to teach youth to say no to drugs and to the friends who may want them to use drugs. The Los Angeles Unified School District and the Los Angeles Police Department developed the DARE program in 1983. In 1986 the US Congress passed the Drug-Free Schools and Communities Act to promote drug abuse education and prevention programs across the country, and DARE spread like wildfire. By 1994 DARE was the most widely used school-based drug prevention program in the country. It was used in all fifty states and spread to foreign countries.

The far reach of DARE would have been great, if the program worked. But it didn't. Research found that DARE graduates were more likely than others to drink alcohol, smoke tobacco, and use illegal drugs. The study asserted that DARE actually increased student drug awareness so that as they got a little older, they became curious about the drugs they had learned about in the program. In 2001 the US surgeon general placed DARE in the category of Ineffective Primary Prevention Programs. In addition, the US General Accountability Office concluded in 2003 that the program was counterproductive in some populations, with DARE graduates having higher than average rates of drug use. Other studies, however, support the effectiveness of new versions of DARE, and the program is still used in the United States and overseas.

incarceration doesn't make society safer—it simply makes offenders "twice as bad."

CONCLUDING THOUGHTS

As JDAI, the Missouri Model, and other evidence-based programs in the United States have demonstrated, secure detention has not worked for youth offenders. Instead, successful programs are those that try to meet the complex needs of individual young people, helping them to succeed in school, at work, with substance abuse and other chronic issues, and in their relationships with others. When I talked to students in Minnesota who were preparing to leave the County Home School, I joked that I hoped I would never see them again. (I also worked with adults in a county correctional facility and often visited adult prisons, where juveniles can end up.) Every resident said, "You won't!" And all of them probably believed it. A decade ago, their chances of breaking that promise were high. These days, with the myriad reforms in the juvenile justice system, these young people have opportunity, not incarceration, in their future.

SOURCE NOTES

4 Dana Canedy, "Sentence of Life without Parole for Boy, 14, in Murder of Girl, 6," *New York Times*, March 10, 2001, http://www.nytimes.com/2001/03/10/us /sentence-of-life-without-parole-for-boy-14-in-murder-of-girl-6.html.

8 "Juvenile Detention Alternative Initiative," Hennepin County, accessed April 12, 2016, http://www.hennepin.us/residents/public-safety/juvenile-detention-alt -initiative.

9–10 James B. Elrod, "Testimony of a Juvenile Offender, Part 1," *LA Progressive*, April 17, 2015, https://www.laprogressive.com/juvenile-offender/.

10 "Youth Incarceration in the United States," available online at National Governor's Association, accessed April 12, 2016, http://www.nga.org/files/live/sites/NGA/ files/pdf/2014/1409LearningLabYouthIncarcerationInfographic_Brown.pdf.

11 Sam Dillon, "Study Finds High Rate of Imprisonment among Dropouts," *New York Times*, October, 8, 2009, http://www.nytimes.com/2009/10/09 /education/09dropout.html?_r=1.

11 Hannah Levintova, "Girls Are the Fastest Growing Group in the Juvenile Justice System," *Mother Jones*, October 1, 2015, http://www.motherjones.com /politics/2015/09/girls-make-ever-growing-proportion-kids-juvenile-justice- system.

18 "The History of Juvenile Justice," American Bar Association, pt. 1, accessed April 4, 2016, http://www.americanbar.org/content/dam/aba/migrated/publiced /features/DYJpart1.authcheckdam.pdf.

20 *The Wild One*, directed by László Benedek, produced by Stanley Kramer (Hollywood, CA: Columbia Pictures, 1953).

21 *In Their Own Words: Young People's Experiences in the Criminal Justice System and Their Perceptions of Its Legitimacy* (Chicago: John Howard Association of Illinois, 2014), 15, http://thejha.org/sites/default/files/JHAInTheirOwnWords.pdf.

22–23 "Kent v. United States," *Legal Information Institute*, accessed April 4, 2016, https://www.law.cornell.edu/supremecourt/text/383/541.

23 *Amendments to the Constitution of the United States of America* (Washington, DC: GPO, 1992), https://www.gpo.gov/fdsys/pkg/GPO-CONAN-1992/pdf/GPO -CONAN-1992-7.pdf.

24 Ibid.

24 "In re Gault," *Legal Information Institute*, accessed April 8, 2016, https://www.law .cornell.edu/supremecourt/text/387/1.

27 "Juvenile Justice and Delinquency Prevention Act of 1974," House Office of the Legislature Counsel, October 9, 2012, http://legcounsel.house.gov/comps /juvenile.pdf.

28 Ed Pilkington, "Jailed for Life at Age 14: US Supreme Court to Consider Juvenile Sentences," *Guardian*, March 19, 2012, http://www.theguardian.com/law/2012 /mar/19/supreme-court-juvenile-life-sentences.

28 Ibid.

31 Richard A Mendel, *No Place for Kids: The Case for Reducing Juvenile Incarceration* (Baltimore: Annie E. Casey Foundation, 2011), 2.

32 Claire Gordon, "After More Than Two Decades in Prison, Another Chance," *Al Jazeera America*, November 13, 2013, http://america.aljazeera.com/watch/shows /america-tonight/america-tonight-blog/2013/11/13/sentenced-to -lifeinprisonasachildadolfodavisgetssecondchance.html.

34 Arne Duncan, "Investing in Teachers Instead of Prisons," US Department of Education, September 30, 2015, http://www.ed.gov/news/speeches/investing-teachers-instead-prisons.

39 Jason Garcia, "New Law Revamps State Boot Camps," *Orlando (FL) Sentinel*, June 1, 2006, http://articles.orlandosentinel.com/2006-06-01/news /BOOTCAMP01_1_boot-camps-martin-ammonia.

40 Meredith Blake, "The Exchange: R. Dwayne Betts on Prison, Poetry, and Justice," *New Yorker*, November 30, 2010, http://www.newyorker.com/books/page-turner /the-exchange-r-dwayne-betts-on-prison-poetry-and-justice.

41 Matt Smith, "Large Youth Prisons Inherently Prone to Abuse, Casey Says," *Juvenile Justice Information Exchange*, July 29, 2015, http://jjie.org/previous-reforms-of-old -model-youth-prisons-eventually-fail-casey-says/.

45 *In Their Own Words.*

49 "Juvenile Detention Alternatives Initiative in Johnson County, Kansas," YouTube, 7:04, posted by "Johnson County, KS," January 13, 2014, http://www.youtube .com/watch?v=Rakt6C_OfoI.

49 Ibid.

49 Ibid.

52 Tim Wu, "Fifty-Five Bodies, and Zero Trials, at the Florida School for Boys," *New Yorker*, January 30, 2014, http://www.newyorker.com/news/news-desk/fifty-five -bodies-and-zero-trials-at-the-florida-school-for-boys.

53 John Maki, "Field Notes: 'You Are Conscious, but You Are Not Intelligent," *Juvenile Justice Information Exchange*, October 9, 2014, http://jjie.org/field-notes -you-are-conscious-but-you-are-not-intelligent/.

54 Eduardo Porter, "Wall St. Money Meets Social Policy at Rikers Island," *New York Times*, July 28, 2015, http://www.nytimes.com/2015/07/29/business/economy /wall-st-money-meets-social-policy-at-rikers-island.html?_r=0.

56 "Ralph Brazel," Sentencing Project, accessed March 15, 2016, http://sentencingproject.org/template/person.cfm?person_id=270.

58 Cicero, *De Legibus*, bk. 3, 20, *Bartle by . com*, accessed April 12, 2016, http://www .bartleby.com/78/668.html.

58 William Blackstone, "Of the Person Capable of Committing Crimes," *Commentaries on the Laws of England (1765–1769),* bk. 4, chap. 2, Lonang

Institute, accessed April 5, 2016, http://lonang.com/library/reference/blackstone
-commentaries-law-england/bla-402/.

60 "Inside Juvenile Prison: What It's Like #2," YouTube, 16:28, posted by
"Calamari Productions," February 9, 2012, https://www.youtube.com/
watch?v=ihk5N5rHy7A.

60 "Inside Juvenile Prison: What It's Like," YouTube, 6:24, posted by
"Calamari Productions," January 22, 2010, https://www.youtube.com/
watch?v=Vjn59b7veGE.

62 Task Force on Community Preventive Services, "Effects on Violence of Laws and
Policies Facilitating the Transfer of Youth from the Juvenile to the Adult Justice
System," *Morbidity and Mortality Weekly Report*, November 30, 2007, 8.

65 "State of South Carolina v. George Stinney, Jr.," State of South Carolina, County
of Clarendon, Third Judical Circuit Court, December 17, 2004, https://www
.scribd.com/fullscreen/250402251.

66 *Amendments to the Constitution.*

67 "Thompson v. Oklahoma," *Legal Information Institute*, accessed April 5, 2016,
https://www.law.cornell.edu/supremecourt/text/487/815.

67 Ibid.

67 "Atkins v. Virginia," *Legal Information Institute*, accessed December 19, 2015,
https://www.law.cornell.edu/supct/html/00-8452.ZO.html.

69 "Roper v. Simmons," *Legal Information Institute*, accessed April 5, 2016, https://
www.law.cornell.edu/supct/html/03-633.ZS.html.

70 "Sara Kruzan: Sentenced to Life without Parole at Age 16," YouTube, 6:08,
posted by "Joseph vbui," February 28, 2009, https://www.youtube.com/
watch?v=qR7mno6p9iQ.

70 Liliana Segura, "16-Year Old Got Life Without Parole for Killing Her Abusive
Pimp—Should Teens Be Condemned to Die in Jail?," *AlterNet,* October 30, 2009,
http://www.alternet.org/story/143635/16-year_old_got_life_without_parole_for_
killing_her_abusive_pimp_--_should_teens_be_condemned_to_die_in_jail.

71 "Graham v. Florida," Supreme Court of the United States, October 2009, http://
www.supremecourt.gov/opinions/09pdf/08-7412.pdf.

71 "Miller v. Alabama," Supreme Court of the United States, October 2011, http://
www.supremecourt.gov/opinions/11pdf/10-9646g2i8.pdf.

71 Yunjiao Amy Li, "In Their Own Words, Inmates Discuss the Riddle of Juvenile
Justice," *Juvenile Justice Information Exchange*, October 14, 2014, http://jjie.org
/in-their-own-words-inmates-discuss-the-riddle-of-juvenile-justice/.

72 Nicholas Williams, "Behind Bars: Four Prison Teens Tell Their Stories," *L.A. Youth*,
February 10, 2016, http://www.layouth.com/behind-bars-four-teens-in-prison
-tell-their-stories/.

74 "Locking Up Fewer Children," *New York Times*, August 13, 2009, http://www
    .nytimes.com/2009/08/14/opinion/14fri3.html?_r=0.

79 "Restorative Justice Practices: Conference Story & Reflection," YouTube, 9:32,
    posted by "IIRP Grad School," April 8, 2014, https://www.youtube.com
    /watch?v=cRJqq0u5hB4.

79 "Victim Offender Reconciliation Program (VORP)," Restorative Justice Partners,
    accessed December 13, 2015, http://www.restorativejusticepartners.com
    /rjpartners/programs/victim-offender-reconciliation-program.

83 Michael W. Hoskins, "Teens Share Stories about Their Juvenile Justice
    Experience," *Indiana Lawyer*, May 14, 2008, http://www.theindianalawyer.com
    /teens-share-stories-about-juvenile-justice-experience/PARAMS/article/24023.

84 Richard Mendel, *Two Decades of JDAI: From Demonstration Project to National
    Standard; A Progress Report* (Baltimore: Annie E. Casey Foundation, 2009), 33.

84 "Dolphy—An IF Team Member Shares His Story," IF Project, May 5, 2015, http://
    www.theifproject.com/2015/05/dolphy-an-if-team-member-shares-his-story/.

84 "Change for Change: Dolphy's Story," YouTube, 3:06, posted by "Take Part TV,"
    May 15, 2013, https://www.youtube.com/watch?v=rfSv39mXuoY.

85 D. M. Altschuler and R. Brash, "Adolescent and Teenage Offenders Confronting
    the Challenges and Opportunities of Reentry," *Youth Violence Juvenile Justice* 2, no.
    1 (2004); 72.

87 Ashley Nellis and Richard A. Hooks Wayman, *Back on Track: Supporting Youth
    Reentry from Out-of-Home Placement to the Community* (Washington, DC:
    Sentencing Project, 2009), 29.

88 *In Their Own Words.*

91 *Homeless in Minnesota: Youth on Their Own,* (Saint Paul: Wilder Research, 2015),
    http://www.wilder.org/Wilder-Research/Publications/Studies/Homelessness%20
    in%20Minnesota%202012%20Study/Homeless%20in%20Minnesota%20-%20
    Youth%20on%20Their%20Own.pdf.

92 "Chance for Change: Xaviar's Story," YouTube, 3:19, posted by "Take Part TV,"
    March 1, 2013, https://www.youtube.com/watch?v=9eUAHlCQle4.

92 Xaviar McElrath-Beay, "The Light at the End of the Tunnel, *Huffington Post*, last
    modified August 21, 2013, http://www.huffingtonpost.com/xavier-mcelrathbey
    /the-light-at-the-end_b_3480715.html.

92 "ICAN Member Profiles," Campaign for the Fair Sentencing of Youth, accessed
    December 12, 2015, http://fairsentencingofyouth.org/stories-from-ican-members/.

95 Richard Mendel, *The Missouri Model Reinventing the Practice of Rehabilitating
    Youthful Offenders* (Baltimore: Annie E. Casey Foundation, 2010), 37.

95 Ibid.

97 Ibid. Summary Report, 5.

97 Ibid. Summary Report, 15.

98 Georgia Rowe, "Nell Bernstein's *Burning Down the House* to Save the Juvenile Justice System," *San Jose Mercury News*, July 7, 2014, http://www.mercurynews .com/entertainment/ci_26109655/nell-bernsteins-burning-down-house-save -juvenile-justice.

98 "*Burning Down the House* Makes the Case against Juvenile Incarceration," *National Public Radio*, June 4, 2014, http://www.npr.org/2014/06/04/318801651/burning -down-the-house-makes-the-case-against-juvenile-incarceration.

98 Ibid.

98–99 Rowe, "Nell Bernstein's *Burning Down the House.*"

Glossary

adjudicate: to hear, decide, and settle a legal case by a judicial procedure such as a hearing before a judge or a trial

aftercare: programs or services provided to offenders upon release from prison or other detention

behavior modification: a therapy model that works to replace undesired behavior with desirable behaviors. This is done with negative or positive reinforcements, such as food distribution. For example, a person who follows the rules gets more food. Those who fail to do so get less food.

capital crime: a crime, such as murder, that is legally punishable by the death penalty

case management: a collaborative effort among human services workers (such as therapists) and corrections personnel (such as probation officers) to assess, plan, implement, and evaluate services for an individual

collateral consequences: legal restrictions or other sanctions (limits) on an offender after release from detention that have negative impacts, such as being unable to find housing or a job

corporal punishment: any penalty in which physical force is used and is intended to cause pain or discomfort

delinquent: commonly used as part of the phrase "juvenile delinquent" to label someone a troublemaker. In the juvenile justice system, a youth offender is found "delinquent" in the same way an adult is found "guilty" in a criminal trial.

detention: a period of time in which a youth offender is held in custody, often in a locked and secure facility

developmentally appropriate: interacting with youth in a way that correlates with their physical, emotional, and intellectual growth

dispose: to determine, in a juvenile case, the consequence of being found delinquent

disproportionate minority contact: the overrepresentation of minority youth within the juvenile justice system, at higher levels than they are present in the general population

diversion program: an activity that shifts youth from the juvenile justice system and into a supervised program such as community service

due process clause: the section of the Fourteenth Amendment to the US Constitution that prohibits depriving any person of life, liberty, or property without a formal and fair legal procedure

evidence-based practices: in the juvenile justice system, processes that rely on the best available scientific research to make and implement decisions about legal processes, programs for juveniles, and sentencing

evolving standards: in constitutional law, a concept for assessing law as something that changes over time as society changes, rather than being fixed and unchangeable. Scholars, judges, journalists, juries, and other sources help decide what these standards are at any given time.

excluded offenses: crimes that are so serious or so minor that they are, based on state law, automatically removed from juvenile court. The serious cases are heard in adult criminal court.

expunge: to remove a person's criminal history from the public record

faith-based organizations: groups that are based out of a church, mosque, temple, or other religious association and that offer religious components as part of their services to individuals

jurisdiction: the area over which a particular unit of government (city, county, etc.) has authority to impose the law, hear cases, and generally run a legal system

juvenile justice system: all aspects of the government institutions involved in interactions with persons under the age of eighteen who have been arrested by the police. This includes police officers, probation officers, judges, juries, guards, therapists, and social workers.

life without parole: a prison sentence in which the offender has no chance for release

mandatory minimum sentencing: laws that require judges to sentence offenders who have committed specific crimes to a certain amount of time in prison, regardless of the circumstances that surrounded the crime

neuroscience: the study of the human nervous system, including the brain, spinal cord, and networks of nerve cells

offender: in the justice system, a person who has committed or is suspected of committing a crime

offense-based sentencing: laws that require judges to impose a mandatory (required) sentence based on the type of crime an offender is convicted of committing

parole: the release of a correctional inmate before that person's full sentence is served, often for exhibiting good behavior while incarcerated

probable cause: a requirement in the US Constitution that the police show reasonable grounds to make an arrest, to conduct a personal or property search, or to obtain a warrant for arrest

probation: a set amount of time an offender receives instead of incarceration and during which that person must exhibit positive behavior. If the person fails to do so, probation is violated and the person may face incarceration.

progressive movement: a political philosophy that arose in the early part of the twentieth century in which government is viewed as a positive force in finding solutions to social problems. The movement and its political candidates also believed that government must adapt with changing times and change policies to meet the needs of changing populations.

publicly funded–privately run: programs, services, or facilities that receive government tax dollars to do business but are run by private, for-profit companies

queer: a person who does not conform to a distinct and traditional sexual or gender identity

recidivism: a person's relapse into (return to) criminal behavior after receiving punishment for a previous crime

reconciliation: a meeting, often conducted face-to-face, where a victim and offender come together to resolve differences as the final stage of making amends in the restorative justice process

reform movement: the belief, which arose in the first two decades of the twentieth century, that changing the behavior of an offender is more important—and more effective—than punishment

rehabilitation: transforming a prisoner from an offender to a productive member of society. The process involves skill building, schooling, job training, therapy, and treatment for any medical or mental health conditions that lead to unhealthy behaviors.

residential placement: a facility that houses a youth offender outside of that person's home. Such placements may include foster care, shelter care, or serving time in a correctional facility such as a reform school.

restitution payments: money a court orders an offender to pay to a victim or victims or to a government agency for damages caused by that person's criminal act

restorative justice: a process through which an offender—often working with that person's victim or victims—repairs the harm

secure detention facility: a building with guards and locked doors that houses persons arrested for a crime while they are awaiting trial

settlement houses: founded in the nineteenth century and early twentieth century, these organizations provided social programs and services to individuals (adults and youth) to help improve education and increase opportunies for those in need

social programs: activities with the goal of improving the lives of people in need. These programs include job training, funds for food, and reduced medical care costs.

technical violation: misbehavior by an offender on probation or on parole and under supervision that is not a criminal offense and would not otherwise result in arrest. The most common violation is not attending required probation meetings.

therapeutic programs: group or individual counseling, drug treatment, and other types of interventions where a trained therapist works with people to help them change harmful behavior

waive jurisdiction: to remove a youth's case from the juvenile court and try it in adult criminal court

Selected Bibliography

Aarons, John, Lisa Smith, and Linda Wagner. *Dispatches from Juvenile Hall: Fixing a Failing System*. New York: Penguin Books, 2009.

Abrams, Laura S., and Ben Anderson-Nathe. *Compassionate Confinement: A Year in the Life of Unit C*. New Brunswick, NJ: Rutgers University Press, 2013.

Bahena, Sofia, North Cooc, Rachel Currie-Rubin, Paul Kuttner, and Monica Ng, eds. *Disrupting the School-to-Prison Pipeline*. Cambridge, MA: Harvard Educational Review, 2012.

Bartol, Curt R, and Anne M. Bartol. *Juvenile Delinquency and Antisocial Behavior: A Developmental Perspective*. Upper Saddle River, NJ: Pearson Prentice Hall, 2009.

Bernstein, Nell. *Burning Down the House: The End of Juvenile Prison*. New York: New Press, 2014.

Betts, R. Dwayne. *Circumference of a Prison: Youth, Race, and the Failures of the American Justice System*. New York: Penguin, 2014.

Billitteri, Thomas J. *Youth Violence: Are "Get Tough" Policies the Best Approach?* Washington, DC: Congressional Quarterly, 2010.

Bradford, Spike. *Common Ground Lessons Learned from Five States That Reduced Juvenile Confinement by More Than Half*. Washington, DC: Justice Policy Institute, 2013.

Brown, Sarah Alice. *Trends in Juvenile Justice State Legislation 2001–2011*. Denver: National Conference of State Legislatures, 2012.

Butts, Jeffrey A., S. Gordon Bazemore, and Aundra Saa Meroe. *Positive Youth Justice: Framing Justice Interventions Using the Concepts of Positive Youth Development*. Washington, DC: Coalition for Juvenile Justice, 2010.

Dowd, Nancy E. *Justice for Kids: Keeping Kids out of the Juvenile Justice System*. New York: New York University, 2011.

Elrod, Preston, and R. Scott Ryder. *Juvenile Justice: A Social, Historical, and Legal Perspective*. Sudbury, MA: Jones and Bartlett, 2011.

Gold, Jerome. *Paranoia & Heartbreak: Fifteen Years in a Juvenile Facility*. New York: Seven Stories, 2009.

Greenwood, Peter W. *Evidence-Based Practice in Juvenile Justice: Progress, Challenges, and Opportunities*. New York: Springer, 2014.

Griffin, Patrick. *Trying Juveniles as Adults: An Analysis of State Transfer Laws and Reporting*. Washington, DC: U.S. Dept. of Justice, Office of Justice Programs, Office of Juvenile Justice and Delinquency Prevention, 2011.

Henry, Nathan L. *Good Behavior*. New York: Bloomsbury, 2010.

Howell, James C. *A Handbook for Evidence-Based Juvenile Justice Systems*. Lanham, MD: Lexington Books, 2014.

Kim, Catherine Y., Daniel J. Losen, and Damon Hewitt. *The School-to-Prison Pipeline: Structuring Legal Reform*. New York: New York University Press, 2010.

Krisberg, Barry. *Juvenile Justice: Redeeming Our Children*. Thousand Oaks, CA: Sage, 2005.

Kysel, Ian. *Growing Up Locked Down: Youth in Solitary Confinement in Jails and Prisons across the United States*. New York: American Civil Liberties Union, 2012.

Lawrence, Richard, and Mario Hesse. *Juvenile Justice: The Essentials*. Thousand Oaks, CA: Sage, 2010.

Lipsey, Mark W., James C. Howell, Marion R. Kelly, Gabrielle Chapman, and Darin Carver. *Improving the Effectiveness of Juvenile Justice Programs: A New Perspective on Evidence-Based Practice*. Washington, DC: Georgetown University, Center for Juvenile Justice Reform, 2011.

Macallair, Daniel, Mike Males, Dinky Manek Enty, and Natasha Vinakor. *Renewing Juvenile Justice*. Sacramento: Sierra Health Foundation, 2011.

Mays, G. Larry, and Rick Ruddell. *Do the Crime, Do the Time: Juvenile Criminals and Adult Justice in the American Court System*. Santa Barbara, CA: Praeger, 2012.

McShane, Marilyn D., and Franklin P. Williams. *Youth Violence and Delinquency: Monsters and Myths*. Westport, CT: Praeger, 2007.

Mendel, Richard. *Reducing Youth Incarceration in the United States*. Baltimore: Annie E. Casey Foundation, 2013.

Mulvey, Edward P. *Highlights from Pathways to Desistance: A Longitudinal Study of Serious Adolescent Offenders*. Washington, DC: U.S. Dept. of Justice, Office of Justice Programs, Office of Juvenile Justice and Delinquency Prevention, 2011.

National Association of Counties. *Juvenile Detention Reform: A Guide for County Officials*. 2nd ed. Washington, DC: National Association of Counties, 2011.

National Conference of State Legislatures. *Introduction & Overview: Juvenile Justice Guide Book for Legislators*. Denver: National Conference of State Legislatures, 2011.

National Council on Crime and Delinquency. *And Justice for Some: Differential Treatment of Youth of Color in the Justice System*. Oakland: National Council on Crime and Delinquency, 2007.

National Juvenile Justice Network. *Advances in Juvenile Justice Reform: 2009–2011*. Washington, DC: National Juvenile Justice Network, 2012.

———. *The Comeback States: Reducing Youth Incarceration in the United States*. Washington, DC: National Juvenile Justice Network, 2013.

Nellis, Ashley, Richard A. Hooks Wayman, and Sarah Schirmer. *Youth Reentry: Youth Development, Theory, Research and Recommended Best Practices*. Washington, DC: Youth Reentry Task Force, 2009.

Nelson, Douglas W. *A Road Map for Juvenile Justice Reform*. Baltimore: Annie E. Casey Foundation, 2008.

Nocella, Anthony J. *From Education to Incarceration: Dismantling the School-to-Prison Pipeline*. New York: Peter Lang, 2014.

Nurse, Anne. *Locked Up, Locked Out: Young Men in the Juvenile Justice System*. Nashville: Vanderbilt University Press, 2010.

Parsons-Pollard, Nicolle Y. *Disproportionate Minority Contact: Current Issues and Policies*. Durham, NC: Carolina Academic Press, 2011.

Ramsay, Neil A., and Colin R. Morrison. *Youth Violence and Juvenile Justice: Causes, Intervention and Treatment Programs*. New York: Nova, 2010.

Scott, Elizabeth S., and Laurence D. Steinberg. *Rethinking Juvenile Justice*. Cambridge, MA: Harvard University Press, 2008.

Sickmund, Melissa. *Juveniles in Residential Placement, 1997–2008*. Washington, DC: U.S. Dept. of Justice, Office of Justice Programs, Office of Juvenile Justice and Delinquency Prevention, 2010.

Slobogin, Christopher, and Mark R. Fondacaro. *Juveniles at Risk: A Plea for Preventive Justice*. Oxford: Oxford University Press, 2011.

Sutton, John. *Stubborn Children: Controlling Delinquency in the United States, 1640–1981*. Berkeley: University of California Press, 1988.

Ziedenberg, Jason. *You're an Adult Now: Youth in Adult Criminal Justice Systems*. Washington, DC: U.S. Dept. of Justice, National Institute of Corrections, 2011.

Zimring, Franklin E., and David Spinoza Tanenhaus. *Choosing the Future for American Juvenile Justice*. New York: New York University Press, 2014.

FURTHER INFORMATION

BOOKS

Fiction

The list contains a selection of realistic novels (no Maze Runner*) set in the United States and published since 2012.*

Beaudoin, Sean. *Wise Young Fool.* New York: Little, Brown, 2013. Eighteen-year-old Ritchie Sudden finds himself locked in juvenile detention as a direct result of issues related to anger and loss. While inside, he keeps a journal about his time locked up and the events that led to his arrest and incarceration.

Cummings, Priscilla. *The Journey Back.* New York: Dutton Children's Books, 2012. Soon after his fourteenth birthday, Michael Griswald escapes from the Cliffside Youth Detention Center, where he has been incarcerated for his role in a prank that turned into murder. He's desperate to return home to protect the rest of his family from his father's violent raging temper.

Dotson-Lewis, Gloria. *You Got Me Twisted.* East Orange, NY: Wahida Clark Presents, 2012. Makenzie has a temper that gets her into trouble time and again. Hauled in front of a judge, she's sentenced to see a therapist or face spending time in Cook County Juvenile Detention.

Goodman, Shawn. *Kindness for Weakness.* New York: Delacorte, 2013. James is a fifteen-year-old boy from an abusive home who desperately seeks his older brother's love and approval. To do so, he starts pushing drugs for him and suffers the consequences.

Jacobs, Evan. *Self. Destructed.* Costa Mesa, CA: Saddleback, 2014. High school junior Michael's life unravels when he brings a gun to school. With zero tolerance policies in place, one stupid act lands him in prison and then on parole.

Jones, Patrick. *Returning to Normal.* Locked Out series. Minneapolis: Darby Creek, 2015. When Xavier's father returns to Boston after serving ten years in a federal prison, tensions quickly mount and Xavier's anger explodes. Can he get it together, or will he follow in his father's path of life behind bars?

McVoy, Terra Elan. *Criminal.* New York: Simon Pulse, 2013. Eighteen-year-old Nikki's love and devotion to her boyfriend Dee takes a dangerous turn when he involves her in a murder that lands her in prison while Dee walks free.

Neff, Beth. *Getting Somewhere.* New York: Viking, 2012. Four teenaged girls find their time in a progressive juvenile detention facility changes their lives in unexpected ways.

Oakes, Stephanie. *The Sacred Lies of Minnow Bly.* New York: Dial Books, 2015. Minnow sits in her juvenile detention cell accused of murdering a cult leader whom she was supposed to marry. When she refused, the cult chopped off her hands. Is the cell she sits in now any worse that the prison of her past?

Simone, Ni-Ni. *Down by Law*. New York: Dafina Books, 2015. Set in the 1980s, *Down by Law* follows Isis Carter as life deals her bad hand after bad hand, which she compounds by making worse choices that land her in juvenile detention.

Sims, Guy, and Dawud Anyabwile. *Monster: A Graphic Novel*. New York: HarperTeen, 2015. Steve Harmon's story, not as a film script but as a graphic novel, is appropriately told in harsh black-and-white drawings.

Willey, Margaret. *Four Secrets*. Minneapolis: Carolrhoda Lab, 2012. Three middle school girls keep journals about the events that lead to their incarceration.

Nonfiction

Bartos, Judeen. *Teen Residential Treatment Programs*. Detroit: Greenhaven, 2013. This is a collection of essays describing various types of programs such as boot camps, reform schools, and other residential programs.

Betts, R. Dwayne. *A Question of Freedom: A Memoir of Survival, Learning, and Coming of Age in Prison*. New York: Avery, 2009. At the age of sixteen, Dwayne Betts and a friend pulled a carjacking. Caught, quickly tried, and convicted in criminal court, he spent the next eight years in an adult prison. In this autobiography, Betts examines the choices he made that led to his prison time and the better choices he hopes to make upon his release. He realizes that through writing he can redeem himself and look toward a brighter future.

Brezina, Corona. *Frequently Asked Questions about Juvenile Detention*. New York: Rosen, 2011. This is an easy-to-read guide to all aspects of juvenile detention.

Cahill, Thomas. *A Saint on Death Row: The Story of Dominique Green*. New York: Nan A. Talese, 2009. Cahill tells the story of a young man from Houston, Texas, who was tried and quickly convicted of murder. He turned his life around in prison while sitting on death row, but it was too late. Despite numerous appeals and pleas for a retrial, Texas executed Green on October 26, 2004.

Chura, David. *I Don't Wish Nobody to Have a Life Like Mine: Tales of Kids in Adult Lockup*. Boston: Beacon, 2010. A teacher in a New York county penitentiary, Chura saw firsthand the impact of locking up youth in adult facilities. Chura explores the broken lives of damaged young people who made bad choices that led to their incarceration.

Haugen, David M., and Susan Musser. *Juvenile Justice*. Detroit: Greenhaven, 2013. A collection of writings about various aspects of the juvenile justice system includes US Supreme Court opinions, personal narratives, and persuasive essays.

Hubner, John. *Last Chance in Texas: The Redemption of Criminal Youth*. New York: Random House, 2005. Journalist Hubner reports on the work of the Giddings State School in Texas, which houses the most serious youth offenders. Hubner relays the stories of one male and one female inmate as they undergo therapeutic interventions. Unveiling the trauma in each person's past and their feelings of remorse, Hubner chronicles their struggle.

Kuklin, Susan. *No Choirboy: Murder, Violence, and Teenagers on Death Row*. New York: Square Fish, 2014. Four inmates sentenced to die for crimes committed while teenagers tell their stories in their own words. Kuklin also tells the story of a victim's family, as well as that of an attorney working with poor offenders.

Longhine, Laura, and Keith Hefner, eds. *Brick Walls of Justice: Teens Write about Crime, Punishment, and Alternatives*. New York: Youth Communication, 2010. This is a series of first-person accounts of young people detailing encounters with the criminal justice system, from arrest to detention through incarceration, as well as sentencing alternatives and probation.

Murray, Elizabeth A. *Overturning Wrongful Convictions: Science Serving Justice*. Minneapolis: Twenty-First Century Books, 2015. This book for YA readers recounts stories of individuals who served someone else's prison time due to mistaken eyewitness identification, police misconduct, faulty forensic science, poor legal representation, courtroom mistakes, and other factors. Readers learn how science and the legal system can work together to right these wrongs.

Ross, Richard. *Juvenile in Justice*. Santa Barbara, CA: Richard Ross, 2012. This oversize book contains more than 250 compelling photographs of people and places, taken by the author from his more than five years of visiting more than two hundred juvenile detention institutions in thirty-one states.

FILMS

The Central Park Five. DVD. New York: Florentine Films, 2013. Award-winning filmmaker Ken Burns explores a grave injustice caused by racial profiling. In 1989 a young white woman jogger was raped in New York's Central Park. Quickly, five youths of color—four black and one Hispanic—were arrested, waived to adult court, tried, convicted, and sentenced. However, as the documentary reveals, none of them were guilty of the crime. The film explores the men's journey to freedom.

The House I Live In. DVD. New York: Charlotte Street Films, 2012. This documentary looks into the consequences of the war on drugs, resulting in mass arrest and incarceration. It mixes news footage with interviews of those involved in the criminal justice system, including adults and teens doing time for minor drug offenses.

Juvies. DVD. Pacific Palisades, CA: Chance Films, 2004. This film follows a dozen youth offenders, all of whom have been charged as adults, as they await trial at Eastlake Juvenile Hall in Los Angeles. Others involved in the juvenile justice system, as well as academics and advocates, explore the issue of trying youth as adults.

Kids for Cash. DVD. New York: Kino Lorber, 2013. This documentary chronicles the "kids for cash" scandal in Pennsylvania, including interviews with families of offenders and news footage of press coverage.

Making a Murderer. DVD. Los Angeles: Synthesis Films, 2015. This Netflix documentary miniseries follows DNA exoneree Steven Avery, who finds himself and his sixteen-year-old nephew Brendan Dassey the prime suspects in another rape and murder. The series investigates corruption in law enforcement and courtroom bias as well as the factors that lead individuals to criminal behavior.

West of Memphis. DVD. New York: Sony Pictures Classic, 2012. In 1993 three young boys were killed in West Memphis, Arkansas. The police arrested three teenagers who were alleged "Satanists." This label and circumstantial evidence led the three to be convicted. The film explores the efforts to have the verdicts overturned, as well as interviews with those involved in the case, including the three convicted men, who were eventually freed.

Young Kids, Hard Time. DVD. Malibu, CA: Calamari Educational Media, 2011. The Wabash Valley Correctional Facility in Indiana is a prison that houses youth convicted and sentenced as adults. This documentary interviews five offenders, as well as adults, about the plight of youth in adult facilities.

WEBSITES

Beat Within
http://www.thebeatwithin.org/
This is the online version of the print publication created by youth in correctional facilities in 1996. Launched as a six-page magazine for kids to react to the death of Tupac Shakur, *Beat Within* has become a biweekly publication featuring writings and drawing from incarcerated youth in California. The website contains more than a year of print versions, a blog, counselor's corner, and videos.

Campaign for Youth Justice
http://www.campaignforyouthjustice.org
Founded by a parent whose teen's case was waived to adult court, the campaign aims to eliminate trying youth in adult criminal court. The site's blogs, tweets, news posts, and research provide hard data. The section of testimonials from parents and youth are especially powerful.

Coalition for Juvenile Justice
http://www.juvjustice.org/
This is the official website for a nationwide network of state groups that aims to prevent youth from becoming involved in the juvenile justice system. The site contains links to resources around the group's core principles, focus areas, and policy recommendations, as well as blogs, electronic newsletters, and reports about keeping youth out of the system or treating them fairly once in it.

Innocence Project
http://www.innocenceproject.org/
Founded in 1992, the goal of the Innocence Project is to gather DNA and other evidence and to file appeals on behalf of people, including juveniles, who have been wrongly convicted of a crime. The site explores the work of the project. Profiles of pending and successfully resolved cases are included at the site.

Juvenile Detention Alternatives Initiative

    http://www.aecf.org/work/juvenile-justice/jdai/

    This official website for the Annie E. Casey Foundation's Juvenile Detention Alternatives Initiative contains links to reports, research, and other resources related to detention alternatives.

Models for Change

    http://www.modelsforchange.net/index.html

    This website serves as a resource for policy makers, advocates, educators, and others involved in juvenile justice reform. Focus areas on the site include aftercare, evidence-based practices, racial-ethnic fairness, and status offense reform. Each focus area contains links to research, publications, and other resources.

Office of Juvenile Justice and Delinquency Prevention

    http://www.ojjdp.gov/

    In addition to the model programs guide, the official website for the lead US government agency in the area of juvenile justice contains links to reports, research, and statistics. Many publications from the department, including electronic newsletters, are available for free download through this site.

Sentencing Project

    http://www.sentencingproject.org/

    This site offers a collection of research, publications, and advocacy resources for changing sentencing laws in the United States. In addition to juvenile justice, focus areas include racial disparity, mass incarceration, drug policy, and collateral consequences.

Index

Photo Acknowledgments

The images in this book are used with the permission of: Backgrounds: © iStockphoto.com/Jason Lugo (fence); © iStockphoto.com/ spxChrome (paper background); © Tom Ervin/Getty Images, p. 5; © Stocksolutions/Alamy, p. 7; The Granger Collection, New York, p. 15; Art and Picture Collection, The New York Public Library, "New York House of Refuge on Randall's Island," New York Public Library Digital Collections, p. 16; The Granger Collection, New York, p. 17; © Everett Collection Historical/Alamy, p. 19; © cineclassico/Alamy, p. 20; Robert Galbraith/Reuters/Newscom, p. 31; © Jim West/Alamy, p. 35; © Rachel Eliza, p. 40; © Rich Legg/E+/Getty Images, p. 43; AP Photo/Al Hartmann/The Salt Lake Tribune, p. 48; Harvard Art Museums/Fogg Museum, Transfer from the Carpenter Center for the Visual Arts, Social Museum Collection, p. 51; © Nina Berman/ NOOR, p. 52; © Christopher Gregory/The New York Times/Redux, p. 54; Ed Hille/The Philadelphia Inquirer/Newscom, p. 55; © St. Louis Post-Dispatch, p. 55; © Hulton Archive/Getty Images, p.59; © Meggan Hallen/The New York Times/Redux, p. 61; © Laura Westlund/Independent Picture Service, p. 63; © State of South Carolina/Wikimedia Commons (public domain), p. 64; AP Photo/ Lake County Police Department, p. 68; © Scott Olson/Getty Images, p. 73; © Gina Ferazzi/Los Angeles Times/Getty Images, p. 78; © Helen H. Richardson/The Denver Post/Getty Images, p. 79; AP Photo/Mary Altaffer, p. 82; © Nancy Stone/Chicago Tribune/TNS/Alamy, p. 86; © Elbert Chu/Do1Thing.org/Redux, p. 91; The Seattle Times, p. 96.

Cover images: © iStockphoto.com/zodebala (man); © iStockphoto .com/Jason Lugo (fence); © iStockphoto.com/spxChrome (paper background).

About the Author

A former teen librarian, Patrick Jones first published at the age of eight in a professional wrestling newsletter. Since then he has published more than two hundred book reviews, one hundred-plus articles, fifty essays in reference works, twenty novels for reluctant teen readers, nine professional books for teachers and librarians, seven young adult novels, and two nonfiction books.

Jones's most recent series, Unbarred, focuses on teens who have been in custody and how they navigate life once on the outside. Jones knows this population very well. For more than fifteen years, he made regular visits to the Hennepin County Home School and the Hennepin County Juvenile Detention Center to provide library service. As an author, he has visited correctional facilities across the country, from Austin, Texas, to Boston, Massachusetts. Learn more about Jones online at www.connectinya.com and on Twitter at #PatrickJonesYA.